CW00549613

SEEK AND YOU
SHALL FIND

Eden Press

SEEK AND YOU SHALL FIND

Edited by
Rebecca Mee

First published in Great Britain in 1999 by Eden
Press, an imprint of
Penhaligon Page Ltd, Remus House, Coltsfoot Drive,
Peterborough. PE2 9JX

A Catalogue record for this book is available from the
British Library

ISBN 1 86226 558 5

Typesetting and layout, Penhaligon Page Ltd, England.
Printed and bound by Forward Press Ltd, England

Foreword

Seek And You Shall Find is a compilation of poetry, featuring some of our finest poets. This book gives an insight into the essence of modern living and deals with the reality of life today. We think we have created an anthology with a universal appeal.

There are many technical aspects to the writing of poetry and *Seek And You Shall Find* contains free verse and examples of more structured work from a wealth of talented poets.

Poetry is a coat of many colours. Today's poets write in a limitless array of styles: traditional rhyming poetry is as alive and kicking today as modern free verse. Language ranges from easily accessible to intricate and elusive.

Poems have a lot to offer in our fast-paced 'instant' world. Reading poems gives us an opportunity to sit back and explore ourselves and the world around us.

Contents

A Thousand, Thousand

Who knows a thousand, thousand
Millennia unaccountable in the passing time
As the stars are stilled to our gaze
Revolve in tumult, we seek peace.
Time does not count our wayward
Glance nor accumulate our vision.
All is past or present or never remembered
Unknown for those that seek the sum
Of our knowledge.

A thousand years ago those prayed
With such reverence for so new a time
For a second dawning, today seek the awning
On the houses God made and tears or smiles
Cannot greet that morning.
Some know the scriptures cannot lie
And light must dispel our constant dread
Of such life in the living and the dead
A life beyond the wordly round where all live
In Truth and none may fall or fail beyond recall.

Much are we taught, a few would know
How our memory of these twice hundred hundred years
Was formed and upon whose life we still seek
The thousand thousand more
Not to forget what man can do to kill a beginning
In what was truly sinning.
In bright vision of that day.

John Amsden

Thoughts On The Millennium

Let the people sing of Jesus
As we celebrate his birth;
He who from self-seeking frees us
Living, dying showed our worth.
We who labour for a living
Let us show him at his trade
Glory to the Father giving
By the easy yokes he made.

Tell the story to the nations
Of his Jordan call to serve,
Of his wilderness temptations
Testing strength of will and nerve.
Show the keenness of his teaching
To the crowds beside the sea
And his ministry of preaching
Through the towns of Galilee.

Sing his mighty acts of healing,
Lame and leper, dumb and blind,
By his active love revealing
God's free grace for all mankind.
Tell how, though the people sought him.
Pharisee and Sadducee
Criticised, condemned and brought him
To a cross on Calvary,

Sing how though men scorned God praised him
Set his seal upon his Word
When with mighty power he raised him
Making him both Christ and Lord.
He is with us as we labour,
Source of faith and hope restored.
By our love for God and neighbour
Ever be his name adored.

Ken French

God

A bright idea,
like a candle
in the dark,
blown out
of all proportion.

S Cardno

The Year 2000 And Beyond

Beyond 2000 we are looking into the unknown,
We cannot see the enigmas of time
Or what hidden secrets lie within the universe
Beyond our wildest dreams sublime.

We live with hope of wars unknown
Where poverty and hunger then will cease
With faith in God those dreams could be reality
And everyone would know a world of peace.

Is that too much to ask of our creator?
I think not - if we love the world as he does,
But everyone must join their hands together
And leave their sins behind them in the dust.

We seek the days of joyfulness
When all families shew endearment
To their offsprings in their need
Instead of gross resentment.

In the year 2000 and beyond
The world may change its shape
We cannot visualise what God will do
Or what changes he will make.

But then again man's ruthlessness
Could leave this world destroyed
Then God would shew no mercy
To those who made it void.

But the Lord is merciful and kind
To those who understand
What love and life, faith and hope
Can mean in this troubled land.

Eileen Chamberlain

4

A Very Special Year

Millennium Song
This poem has been set to music by the author.
She will be singing it at various venues over
the millennium period.

Are we losing the message of Christmas?
Is this a very special year?
Are we forgetting how it all started?
Is there a voice we just don't hear?
Shepherds in the fields were waiting;
Wise men travelled from afar,
Mary's child in a stable was sleeping
Far below that shining star.

Christians know that the *word* has been spreading
Two thousand years, through all mankind.
Do we receive it and see the *light* shine,
Or have we chosen to be blind?
At this time we should be giving,
Not just gifts, but time and love.
Let us experience the joy of living,
With God's Blessing from Above.

We shall discover the message of Christmas
This is a very special year.
We shall remember how it all started,
Singing with voices loud and clear!

Marjorie Holmes

Millennium 2000

This Millennium year is just eight months away
Let's hope it's a future period of peace
And happiness, for ever and a day.

1999 has been a year of problems and
Tribulations, both in politics and
Everyday occurrences, and cannot
Be denied.
Surely this world of ours is big enough
For all to live peacefully side-by-side.

But man, at times, has decided otherwise
Bringing chaos, casualties and concern
To one and all
Now we must look forward to the start
Of this very special festive year
Ahead - memories we will recall
So
Let's celebrate, in style, and be proud
To be British - through and through.
A happy and successful 'Millennium'
Year to all of you.

J Greenacre

The Garden Of Faith

When you walk in the garden of loneliness, let faith be your
                                                    guide,
For troubles rise like shadows, the paths are steep, and wide,
When all you see are mountains, and clouds around you creep,
The heart is heavy, and silent tears you weep,
Then faith takes a hand, and lulls the soul to sleep,
Perversity, discouragement, the moods of despair
Vanish, with a dawn so clear, you can taste the mountain air,
For the love of God has found you, surrounded you with His love
And the doves of peace on you descend, from His Kingdom
                                                    above.

Dorothy Ronald

Christian Millennium

On this Millennium morning
We celebrate a birth
A birth in that fair city
Of the Saviour of the world.

During this Millennium
We have suffered many things
We suffered plague and warfare
Holocaust and fear.

Yet our Saviour born so long ago
Has guided to this day
Guided us to look for peace
As never such before.

We are much more aware today
(Than 1000 years ago)
That only peace amongst our lands
Can satisfy our needs.

We thank God for this Millennium
This God who first loved us
We thank him for his time on earth
And for the promise of a better life
With him, whose birth we celebrate.

We celebrate the birth of Christ
On this Millennium Day
We thank him for our own birthday
Our welcome on this earth.
We welcome him who first loved us
And loves us evermore.

Janet Cavill

I've Stood At His Cross

Over and over, I've felt all life's pain.
Over and over, felt life was in vain;
Over and over, I've stood at 'His' Cross,
And it made me realise what I have lost:
Nothing, in fact. For all is on loan:
Nothing goes with us when we are called home.
Each situation, a new-coloured leaf
To add to this body that carries my grief,
A body that aches with pain and despair,
A body that copes when trouble is there;
The house which I live in, the house of my soul,
A flesh-covered house which takes full control
Of each situation or leaf on my branch:
This tree of my life grows way in advance,
It travels before me, as Nature with Seasons.
And, ask as we might, what are the reasons
For suffering and anguish, for all life's despair
And days when there's pain and nobody cares.
But autumn is sadness, and all leaves must go;
And winter is healing, where each of us grow.
And spring is a smile to brighten our face,
And summer is fullness for the body's own grace.
And so with the tree as with our own life:
Nature and man experiencing strife.
Is it all worth it? We'll find out one day.
When we go to that home where no cross is displayed,
For it has been left here. It no longer has use,
For Heaven requires no earthly proof
That suffering is over, that pain is all done:
That house is now empty, that flesh-troubled one.
We rise as a spirit, as we fall in the flesh;
God has His reasons for what seems just a mess:
The cross, it was earth-made and so is our pain;
Thank God there's a Heaven where peace does remain.

Kathleen Y Ambler

9

Harvest Thanksgiving

We are here to give our thanks
For the harvest once again.
If we care for your good earth
You will always give rebirth,
To the seed which has been sown,
Cared and tended it has grown,
Till the harvest time we see
And we turn our thoughts to thee.

You the Giver of Increase
We partake of the feast.
Let us always thankful be
For the gifts that come from thee.
Beauty all around to see
Singing birds that are so free,
Eyes to see, and ears to hear
Showing us that you are near.

Nearer to us every day
As we walk along your way
On the street and on the field
If to you our wills we yield,
Then the hungry will be heard
All good gifts have come from you
Bless us when we are givers to.

Another harvest there will be
When He calls "Come unto me"
Let us hear your Sacred Voice,
And with willing hearts rejoice
All our sins He's washed away
As He suffered on that Day,
Heavenly Father may we be
Workers in the fields for thee.

J G Richards

The Lighthouse

Like a lighthouse
watches over the ocean,
So my spirit has been set free.

So this lighthouse
Watches over the ocean,
Keeping big rocks away from me.

For Jesus is my lighthouse;
His glowing light protects
In times of destitute and trouble
It's us that he selects.

Thank you, magnificent lighthouse
Thank you for watching me;
A ship's been anchored in now
Your love has set me free.
        Amen.
                (John 8:12)

S Spencer

Sacrifices

In many ways in life we see
How people give of themselves, so free.
Some sacrifices are big, some small
Some folk give of their very all.

The parents who have scrimped and saved, that to their
child could give.
The best of education, that a full life they might live
The daughter who has stayed at home, to look after
mum or dad.
In doing so, no life herself has had.

We think of fireman, policeman too, who often are
so brave.
They give their own lives, that others they might save.
The dockers, and the nurses, who many hours do spend.
In hospitals and visiting homes, as our illnesses they
tend.

Have you ever watched a mother hen protect her little
brood.
When she saw they were in danger, firm, and straight
she stood.
The dog who protects his master, or his mistress too.
He will lay down his life for them, his loyalty so true.

Most of us, can look back in our lives, and see
How on certain occasions we have our services given free.
That others might benefit, we try with all our might.
To the best of our ability, to rescue them from their plight.

As we think of these sacrifices, large or small.
There is the one great sacrifice, the greatest of all
When God sent down His only son, on this earth to live.
And if people would listen, Eternal life to give.

Then Jesus died upon the cross, on the hill at Calvary.
He hung there, and He suffered that we might be made
$$\text{free.}$$
He made that great sacrifice, to save us from our sin.
How sad when we reject Him, into our lives won't let
$$\text{Him in.}$$

As we think about sacrifices, how brave people can be.
How much love shown to one another through these we see.
That great love, when God gave for us His son.
Let us show this love to all we meet that His will may be done.

E Griffin

Alchemist Divine

Down I came from the mountain top.
Down from the Lord's high place.
With angel voices in the air,
And the rain mist on my face.
Banished was the clash of violence,
Scattered were earth's evil men;
Shaken out like a blanket, never more to hold
                                    power again.
I saw the lamb, and lion, led by some little child.
Where roses bloomed, with the myrtle tree.
Over land once desert wild.
Gathered together were the nations,
Healed by the light of truth;
Their faces shone like some celestial host;
For they wore the robes of eternal youth.
Freed was this world from evil.
As the ancient seers had foretold of old.
The glory of the Lord, shone over all,
For earth's dross had turned to gold.

John Clarkson Taylor

God's Eyes

God does not look at the colour of our skin
He looks beneath the flesh to see what lies within
The colour of our Soul, is it Black, or White, or Grey.
And what is written on it, what has it to say
I am not my Body, my Body is not me
I am my Soul and Spirit, only Death can set me free.
But whilst I'm on Earth, I must do the Best I can
To make life a little easier for our Fellow Man
So help me Dear God, in your Own Special Way
To pick up my Feet, when they Stumble and Stray
And my Soul will show at the Very End
You are my Salvation, my King and my Friend.

Sophie Godfrey

New World

Peace and friendship is the answer, not only to us on earth but to our brothers above.

Oh for the insight to see
The future of our earth and all that be
Will brother love brother throughout time (*and sister*)
Can peace and friendship prevail

Or will war and destruction lay waste this land
Will brother kill brother throughout our reign
Will we ever know our true worth (*the meaning of life*)
That love and peace is the answer to lie, we are all the same

God created man so you see (*and woman*)
To live together and all that be (*all life on earth*)
So why not take a lesson from the one who is high (*our creator*)
And learn to live together before we all die (*nuclear holocaust*)

Think of our children and their children too
It is really up to me and you (*worldwide*)
Make this earth a better place to live (*for all of mankind*)
With peace and love we can all share and give

When we meet our maker (*our creator*) he will greet us with a smile
He will sit down with us and talk for a while
The glory of heaven waits for you
You have done what the holy book has told you to
                                    (*ten commandments*)

Time on earth is nearly at an end
Then down from heaven to earth my angels I will send
                                    (*Our spacebrothers*)
To call all righteous people by my side
The living, and all who have died
To rule with me over this land (*new earth*)
With peace and love, finally hand in hand (*the final conquest of evil*)

K Jones

16

Lord Here I Stand

Here I stand
Watching the skies more
Standing here waiting
Here for your coming.

Lord your face looking down here
Seeing your children.
I meet people seeing your
Work seeing your work
Being done.

I'm seeing
Men and ladies being touched
By your hands.

Deborah Hepworth

I Am The Living Bread

Jesus - the bread
Of which we eat
Ourselves a chrysalis
Become a butterfly
A certain death
A certain time of waiting
And then again the question
Do you serve?

Jesus - the bread,
For God is Living -
Christ the Way
The Medium
The work is done
Christ died for us

But we in co-operation
Must play our part
A Holy Thing
Made Holy
By the royal Mass

In Christ's Giving
The world received.
In his giving the bread
We receive
But it is to the
Offering made on our part

If this is real
Then it is ours
Or if not
then a cold dead thing on our part.

Christ the Vine
To Him we live.

We are not alive
Not Christian
If this is not entered into.

If God it is, who leads us
Then, our chrysalis shed,
We emerge -
But we cannot see the glory
Not yet. That is to come.

Hazel Smith

Harvest Time

Seasons come and seasons go
Life changes as time speeds by
Nature surprises us with each new day
Our lives to bless and beautify

Farmers busy, ploughing, filling
Seeds of grain in new turned earth
With eager hopes of reaping later
Crops of greatest size and worth

In gardens big and gardens small
With love the seeds are planted
Old soil renewed with tender care
Then fruits by God are granted.

Then comes the time for harvesting
To gather in the store
Of all the blessings God has given
Enough for all, and even more

In field and meadow ripened corn
Barley, oats and wheat
Assuring us that all next year
We'll have enough to eat

In orchards too, the fruit abounds
The trees are bending low
With apples, cherries, pears and plums
We marvel just to see them so

On trees and hedgerows berries bright
In profusion grow
Giving birds their food supply
From tiny wren to big black crow.

Whatever else in life may change
A promise God did make
That Harvest time shall never cease
And He will ne'er forsake

Now as we start another year
Ploughing, tilling, sowing
We feel assured that all those seeds
In season will be growing

Another harvest to be reaped
To reward us for our labours
Food in plenty, enough for us
And all our friends and neighbours.

F M Cater

The Lord Is Near

O Lord, I feel your presence
In the peaceful countryside.
In the bleating of the sheep and lambs
Grazing side by side.
In the lowing of the cattle
As they wander over the lea,
O Lord, I feel your presence
And the love you offer me.

O Lord, I hear you speaking
Through the singing of a bird.
Above the trickling of a stream
Again your voice is heard.
And in the rustling of the trees
When wind disturbs the air.
O Lord, I hear you speaking
Your voice is everywhere.

O Lord I feel you near me
On the noisy busy street.
Amid the rushing traffic
Or the tired trudging feet,
In the hustle and the bustle
Of people passing by
O Lord, I hear you whisper
Saying 'Listen, here am I.'

O Lord be ever near me
In the stillness of the night
O Lord be ever near me
Change my darkness into light.
O Lord, speak Thou within me
In thy loving tender voice,
That I may know your presence
And in your love rejoice.

F C Bonfield

A Heavenly Walk

Have you ever walked the dales
When the trees seem black
And the breeze is a gentle rhythm on your back,
When the sun has set and the evening is dark
And the heathlands quiet from the sound of the lark
The circular moon sheds it beams o'er a hill
Your wonderful world is quiet and still
The only sounds that one can hear
Are the distant sounds which are held so dear
To people in a material age,
Who kneel in homage to wealth and wage.
But to walk through the dales at the end of the day
When the clouds brush the moon
Whilst you joyfully lose your way
Are treasures in heaven beyond great price
For this stillness is *the master's voice*

Be still and know that I am God *Psalm 46 v 10*

Alan Lucas

23

I'm A Christian?

I'm the best Christian that you've ever seen
I go to my church every Sunday
I murmur the prayers and sing all the hymns -
That's the Sabbath all done with - now - Monday.

I'll do my washing, perhaps the ironing too
There's a film on that I'd like to see
It will pass a few hours till the family comes home
and then I'll be cooking the tea.

In the evening there'll be another good film
I can watch till it's time for bed
Then up the stairs, another day gone
I'll sleep when a short prayer I've said.

All the week passes by in like fashion
Till at last it's Sunday again.
Being a good Christian then, off I will go
to church - then - more of the same.

But - was this what the Lord Jesus taught
when He spoke about loving your brothers?
Did He mean just church on Sundays,
and the rest of the week - blow the others?

No - this isn't the message that Jesus gave
about living the Christian life
This isn't the way to earn our crown
and gain eternal life!

We should treat every day like Sunday,
remembering the Lord all the time.
We should think more of others and less of ourselves,
and - reading the Bible's no crime!

Well - maybe I'm not the best Christian you've seen
I shouldn't hold my head high
I should bow it more often in prayer to my Lord -
Forgive me Father - I'll try -

To be a good Christian, and never, with pride,
Point to the things I've done
But remember the things I didn't do -
For the sake of Jesus - your Son!

Pat McKinstry

Your Love

Your love
must be so
great for me
To suffer death
at Calvary.
You could have lived so full a life
With power and money, home and wife.
You could have travelled, seen the world,
Been a father, with boy and girl.
You could have conquered lands and
kings,
Have done and had everything.
And yet, O Son of God, you chose
To sacrifice all this, because
Your love for me was greater than
All these and more in God's great plan.

Chris Murray

Rain

Splash, Splash, goes the rain.
It falls from the clouds.
I love stamping in the puddles.
Is it blue or is it white?
Rain, rain, I hate the rain. Do you?
I have my umbrella, but it never rains.
Sometimes it is very bad.
It rains, it is lightning and it thunders.
Rain, rain, is wet and rain is water.
Rain goes in the drain.
Then it goes into the gutters like a waterfall.
The sun shines and the water goes up into the clouds.
The clouds get heavy.
The rain goes down and down to the ground.
Then the sun shines down and it does this again and again.
Then it turns into a *rainbow.*

Catherine Rossides (5)

Come, Follow Me

My Lord led me up a very high hill
Till we came to some level ground.
And then, when the air was clear and still,
He asked me to look around.
He showed me the plains with the flowers and trees,
The rivers, with waters so bright,
A straight path, where one could walk with ease,
Bathed in the warm sunlight.

He asked me if I would walk with Him there,
And I answered yes, without a care.

The scenery changed, the light grew dark,
The pathway fell away,
To a rocky track through countryside stark,
And the air was cold and grey,
And as I looked on that desolate land,
My heart was touched with fear.
But quietly He asked, while He held my hand,
Would I also walk with Him here?

Though faltering now, I still replied
I would go if He was by my side.

A crossroad now, no sun nor rain,
No light nor darkness here,
An emptiness, no joy, no pain.
The way ahead unclear.
To turn back just was not a choice,
But where did this path lead?
I listened for that still small voice,
A promise, to meet my need.

But His only words were 'Follow me!'
And His silence met my uncertainty.

Surely this was the hardest path of all,
I could not go this way!
I reasoned I had misheard His call,
And that at the crossroads I'd stay.
How could I follow where I could not see?
Without even the touch of His hand.
And still He called me, persistently,
Not waiting that I understand.

He asked if I'd follow by faith, not by sight,
And in answering yes, my heart grew light!

Janet Wood

Untitled

The world goes on about us,
I can hear its cry,
But the stillness in the garden
Was made for you and I.

All I hear are footsteps,
Though the traffic rumbles by,
And the beauty of the garden
Was made for you and I.

There is life here in abundance
That the world cannot descry.
The perfection of the garden
Was made for you and I.

Alison Jacobs

Some Lives

(A tribute to Diana, Princess of Wales and Mother Teresa of Calcutta)

Some lives are short and full of hope, and packed with expectation,
A mixture of good motherhood, yet sad anticipation.
Such was Diana's chosen lot, her kindness shown to many;
A princess with a human trait - just the same as any.
She's left her mark, now may her sons find comfort as they know
The work she started in God's name in future years will grow.

Some lives are long and full of love, with holiness are blessed
In caring for the dying, the homeless and oppressed.
Teresa of Calcutta, a Mother to them all
Gave up her creature comforts in answer to God's call.
Her ministry of healing, of prayer and dedication
Brought her recognition from every kind of nation.
She gained the Nobel Peace award and founded a new order.
Her sisters went to every land of poverty and disorder.
The work she started in God's name is there for all to see,
For in her life she was a saint and in her death will be.

Joyce Pow

A Christmas Card For Annie

Dear Lord

I'm sitting here alone in the dark
Thinking of old Annie in the park
As she lies there on a bench with no home
If only there was something I could do
To help ease the pain she's been through.
I've known that old lady all my life
She once had a family and a life
Her husband was a loving caring man
Always kept his family close at hand
Often I would see them hand in hand
With their two small children at their side
They looked so proud as they passed me by
She would say hello with a smile that seemed to glow
Then one night as Christmas Day was near
The cries for help I will always hear
At first I thought I was in a dream
Until I heard that poor old lady scream.
As I looked through the window across the street
And seen the lady standing in bare feet
Screaming for her family trapped inside
The house ablaze with nowhere to hide
The loving husband had got old Annie safe
But couldn't leave his children in the blaze
So he died with the children he adored
Leaving dear old Annie on her own
As time went by she couldn't cope alone
Without her loving family and no home
People tried to help but had no joy
Dear old Annie's life had been destroyed
Now old Annie just drifts from place to place
Most of the time in a kind of daze
I often pass her in the park at night
She doesn't really know me at first sight
If only there was something I could do

I could cope with my life better too
The heartache the sadness she's been through
Seems to keep me going through my life too
So I just pray that one day she'll be free
And leave this lonely life of misery
So please Lord when Annie's time has come
Take her in your arms and give her love
And let her see the family that she loved.

Thomas Boyle

Hope

Empire, Monarchy, Structure, History.
A weight to be carried, juggled, wrestled with.
An invisible stricture going through time,
through the moments of today and now.
Gripping with a hand so strong, it wrenches,
squeezes, suffocates and stifles.
Pounding on relentlessly, until the spirit submits,
gives in, dies and dies and is nearly lost
beyond recognition.

Until the day when light pierces the darkness, and
we arise from the ashes and see our true selves,
marred, broken, dirty, scarred, yet intact! and we
slowly move out to a greater awakening
that is yet to come.

Janet Butters

On Looking Down From The Balustrade
At The Entrance To Market Cross Shopping Centre in
Kilkenny

I could not find the words to tell
what a blast of jazz sang from the bowl
and though I failed to break the spell
wanted to shout: Arise my soul!
In childhood I hoped you would be like
this. Light to the Beatles, joyous God!
Now is the time for you to strike
your servant with your conducting rod
and spirit me to that other realm
where trivialities will cease
and I can leave hold of the helm
of my sinking barque, drown in your peace
and explore the music of the deep unknown
a flickering light has quaintly shown.

Brian Power

Forgive Us Our Trespassers

I see the crowds, I hear them roar
I see you stumble to the floor
pick up your cross and carry on.
Oh Jesus mine what have I done?

But that was then and this is now
yet I'm to blame, sweats on my brow.
You suffered so for all my sins.
They stick in nails like big black pins.

The blood drips down my heart is sore
for one pure heart who died before.
Not satisfied they stick a sword
into your side then walk onward.

You're left alone bereft and dry
You ask for water and you cry.
But no-one hears your lonely voice.
You die alone you have no choice.

Some nights I hear your voice so weak
I cry for you so kind and meek.
If I had only seen your plight
been there to comfort on that night.

To warm your feet and give you drink
While into death you gently sink
To bathe your wounds and cover you up
And hold the vessel as you sup.

To sing you songs between my tears
You were so brave you had no fears.
Oh Calvary you cruel hill
You'll haunt me and my nightmares fill.

How could you all have let Him die
Just stood and watched oh why oh why?
My tears fall fast as falling rain
'Oh Jesus please come back again.'

Let me hold and comfort you
Touch your wounds so black and blue.
Let me beg for mercy true,
Whisper words of 'I love you.'

Ann Tasker

Can You Remember?

Can you remember the bliss
Of slipping between cool cotton sheets.
At the end of a long tiring day?
Now, it is this -
The tired, weary body just meets
An airless duvet.

Can you remember the joy
Of a walk on a frosty morn
In the bright sunlight?
Now, you just lie,
Awake and weary, at dawn,
After heat of the night.

Can you remember the smell,
The sweet scent of earth, after rain.
The fragrance of flowers?
Now, with the traffic, as well,
Exhaust fumes again and again,
As they speed by, for hours.

Can you remember awaking
To the dawn chorus song of each bird
And their music the whole day long?
Now, when the dawn is breaking,
Many birds cannot be heard,
Silent their song.

Can you remember folk singing,
Around a piano, they'd meet,
Sweet music 'midst laughter or tears?
Many to us are now bringing
Pounding harsh 'music', with loud beat,
Shattering our ears.

Remember how children used to be free
To wander alone, or climb up a tree,
Or fish in a brook, or climb up a hill.
Not safe for them, always, to be alone, still.

Anyhow, praise God, He is still on His throne,
And His angels watch over us, when we're alone,
So let's count our blessings, every day,
Whatever the changes we find on life's way.

Winifred R Pettitt

Saints

He wears a helmet, a cap or a cowl,
Occasionally commits a professional foul.
She comforts and cares, just a funny old dear,
He wears gold lame and a ring in his ear.

He stands on a soap-box or bangs a big drum,
They are a mundane Dad or Mum.
The Policeman, a shepherd tending his sheep,
A penniless hobo with nowhere to sleep.

He blows a hot trumpet in a Brass Band,
Exists on a diet of parched burning sand.
The face of an angel or ugly as sin,
A dis-spirited loser or certain to win.

Volunteers work because they believe,
It's better to give than ever receive.
A helping hand from a mysterious stranger,
A warning cry when a life is in danger.

A sentry on duty, brave and bold,
Yet a uniform covers a heart of gold.
Arrayed in a variety of subtle disguises,
Remember, saints come in all shapes and sizes!

B E Ison

Cwm Pennant

We met the evening of my stay,
An uninvited guest to home and land.
A brief encounter to be sure.
But one I'll treasure evermore.
'Come, share my grandeur' you seemed to say.
I did,
And fear I fell in love along the way.

Enchanted by your calm untroubled strength,
Your outstretched arms the sheep to gather.
Swallows flying. Sign of better weather.
I listened to the silence of the night.
'I'll come again.' I said.
And prayed I might.

I did return to see you ere I left,
And shared a sunlit day along your banks.
The valley was so quiet I could hear a cuckoo call,
Violets grew along your wayside wall.
The peace and beauty of this place
Overflowed my heart with grace.

How could I leave your lonely spaces?
Your cooling streams and warm embraces?
You looked so lovely in the sun
How could I interrupt your fun?
But time did come, my friend, for us to part.
And I confess,
I stole a portion of your peace to keep within my heart.

Nancy E Kiberd

Triggersfield In Winter

Tinsel-frosted blades of grass,
Sheep like judges calm and passive,
Floppy crows and seagulls pass
Scribbled clouds in spaces massive.

> Mary of Bethlehem, help me to praise!
> Teach me to lift up my soul;
> Show me the face of the Ancient of Days,
> Hid in a stable where animals laze,
> Making humanity whole.

Wiry silhouettes of trees,
Orange squares in windows gleaming;
Slippery path and icy breeze,
Empty goals of hockey dreaming.

> Mary of Magdala, make me repent!
> Show me your love and your grief;
> Point to the steps of the Saviour Who went,
> Searching for lives that were sin-spoiled and spent,
> Bringing release and relief.

Trigger darting here and there,
Nose to ground and tail ecstatic,
Gulping in the ice-cream air;
Rushing back with dash dramatic.

> Mary of Bethany, teach me to pray,
> Sitting with you at His feet.
> Asking His help for the needs of the day,
> Paying attention to all He will say,
> Bringing him people I'll meet.

One last turn and home's in sight;
Evergreens in sombre order
Fling their shadows deeper white,
Where the sun is a marauder.

Jesus of Nazareth, grant us Your peace!

J Chantry

Christmas

Christmas Eve, our fir tree stands all a glitter,
While outside the winds are bitter.
Balloons and paper hats and cakes
Lots of festive things, this season takes.
Wine and puddings to our tummies we employ
All of these to bring us joy.
Do they? No, I doubt it very much,
No real joy from turkey, goose and such.
Christmas may have gifts wrapped and tied with tinsel strings,
But it's not what Christmas really brings.
There's more to it, and I can tell you so
For on this eve, two thousand years ago
A maiden fair, so sweet and mild
Brought forth, for us, a little child.
We know it's Jesus our saviour born,
To die to save us, wounded, torn
But he rose again, he brings us joy
Praise to God for that baby boy.

J Scher

God's Love

His guiding hand and Spirit move in ways we little know.
And yet He gently leads us on and loves us to His throne of grace.

A broken and a contrite heart the Lord will not despise,
How else but through a contrite heart will Jesus make us wise

His word of life is freely given, there are no strings to bind,
His love is never ending love, unselfish love and kind.

For who can say by what strange way Christ brings His will to light,
Or name the gifts He gives each one to help him in his fight.

He watches us, where once He was, now where His Spirit moves.
And guides us gently in the tasks He sets us from above.

His love for little ones is known, He suffers them to come
To His great heart, he holds them close and loses never one.

For God's eternal laws are kind they break those hearts of stone.
And bring poor sinners to their kness before His holy throne.

All praise the Lord for this His work in all of us, His church.
And pray His work may still go on to show His love on earth.

C H Bearpark

The Bridge

My life is like a bridge,
over a raging sea;
One side is where I am,
The other where I'd like to be.

Bits of me in bundles,
laying on one side;
Waiting to be altered,
especially the bundle of pride.

Occasionally I'd unwrap one,
and offer it up in prayer;
I know the lord will help me,
I've no need to despair.

Once I'd made the changes,
I'd set off happily;
To the far side of the bridge,
Where my Lord waits for me.

I don't always make it,
Satan creeps up craftily;
Head down in shame I return,
Feet dragging heavily.

In confession my Priest I'd see,
and my sad story tell;
And when the Lord's forgiven me,
I'd pray and let out a yell.

Satan stay away from me,
the changes will take place;
All bundles will go over that bridge,
and I'll be full of God's own grace.

Eventually I make it,
and I look back with glee;
Over the calm, serene waters,
that was once a raging sea.

The battle now has ended,
My Lord looks after me;
I've made my final journey,
To the side of the bridge I'd rather be!

James Turton

Modern Religions

The great Gods of our time channel all the great and good.
The chosen teams performance grants up elation or dark
                                        despair.
The TV dominates our living space, omnipotent, oblivious
to its homage paid by pale lives unlived, but grants a
mindless escape, to its devotees.
The acolytes gradually fill the right modern structures,
gravely carrying out the procedures of lifted elbow aiding
the sacred brew over the throat. This magic potion gives
brilliance to the conversations which are an integral part
of one of the ceremony. Hail the great God Pub.

What if we don't care for these great social Gods?
Well, there is always the personal Gods of addiction
The little pill to ease the pain, the excitement of the
chase, the gamble whose thrill takes you over the edge,
beyond human concerns. A very jealous God, this.
The needle giving blessed escape from life until it takes
your own. The final promise.
The extra piece of chocolate, comforting a fat body.
We chose the Gods that give meaning to our lives.
Who is yours?

Greta Carty

Holy Trinity One God

Watch over my heart this day
God of love and light.
Keep me always in thy sight
Teach me every hour to love and pray.

Almighty Father take my life
And weld it to thy eternal will.
Bid my soul to hear thee and be still
Through earth's turmoil and its strife.

Eternal son of God, Lord of all mankind,
Word made flesh in Mary's womb,
Through thy birth, through thy cross and empty tomb,
Risen Saviour, fill my mind.

Holy Spirit, guard me with thy grace;
Guide my lips, my sight, my feet,
Living flame and Paraclete,
That I may find all joy before thy face.

Uvedale Tristram

The Way Of The Cross

I call you to walk now the way of the cross
Not looking behind you, or weighing the cost,
Move on step by step, as I give you the strength,
Measuring progress by forward, not length.
Press on, press on towards the prize,
The direction is heavenwards, on that fix your eyes.

The way of the cross is not fortune or fame,
But humility, sacrifice, suffering and shame,
Forsaking all rights for the sake of My name,
Sharing My cup of sorrow and pain.

The way of the cross is a hard road to take
Of loneliness, darkness and knowing heartbreak,
But walking this way is by freedom of choice,
As each one responds to His Master's Voice.

The way of the cross is not pleasure, but pain,
Some things must die for the goal to obtain,
But out of the ashes of death, there will rise
A pearl of great value, on that fix your eyes.

The way of the cross leads to glorious new life,
Jesus the victory, Jesus the prize,
Jesus the name on all lips as you meet,
Jesus as Lord in your homes, in your streets.

I call you to walk now the way of the cross
Not looking behind you, or weighing the cost.
Move on step by step - I will give you the strength,
Measure your progress by forward, not length,
Keep pressing on towards the prize
The direction is Jesus, on Me fix your eyes.

Helen Goldenberg

Seek And Find

All night shines the moon, brilliantly glowing bright.
Surrounded by the stars, like candles all alight.
Before my eyes I close, to gain much needed sleep,
I listen as owls hoot, then they that sound repeat.
They cry as they fly off each one in search of food,
busily they work, near me outside in yonder wood.
I then climb into bed still pondering my day,
for I cannot end it 'til to my God I pray.
So much I have to tell him, I'm glad to be alive,
full of strength he gives me, so I may survive.
Yet so much has occurred which puzzles me anon,
I try to figure out, but answers still won't come.
Difficult should not be, solutions still I crave,
Why *all* are as they are, from cradle to their grave.
When I was a small child, no answers then I sought,
Innocence of youth meant believing what was taught.
When I leave my bed still I'm trying to surmise,
Puzzling in my mind what brain may jeopardise.
Why must things be *like* this, different for everyone.
Each person must for themself, find road to Kingdom come.
Now time has sped along, old age waits by my door,
Have had so many long years, I can't live many more.
I'm shaky and so frail, grim, reaper's here to see,
If I've learned the lessons which God has given me.
Heartbeats start to fail; I stand at Heaven's gate.
Only now I realise and can appreciate,
For suddenly I *know*, do not simply surmise.
All answers I was seeking are with God in the skies.

Barbara Goode

Heaven

I sought the gate of Heaven, I knocked it
was opened wide, I saw a welcome figure who bade
me step inside. A host of angels were singing,
there was joy in every heart.

I'll n'er forget that welcome right at the very
start; Warmth it just came O'er me as I gazed
upon the throng, I heard a voice just whisper,
my friend you now belong.

They led me to the centre, on passing I saw faces
that I knew, each one was filled with Glory! I
knew that mine was too! The place I was in was
peaceful, filled with a light so New!

Oh! The figure in the centre, So bright and so
Holy too! There were millions of Angels singing,
their voices blending so well, the words were
Holy, Holy, my knees felt weak and I fell.

Then a voice called my name and I trembled, 'tis
you I require it said, then I was lifted very
gently, to the figure I was led; I stood in front
of the figure.

So Holy and Bright the scene, my name was called
a second time, it said your robes are clean;
I tried to life my eyes to see, but the Light
was much too bright for me, I was led a little
way on and was told, I had met God's Son. Jesus!

E Sharpley

Our Lord's Sacrifice

Some people go down to Mass Sunday morning
And some people might think it can be very boring.
But the most important thing we go for is
For the body and blood of our Lord Jesus Christ
For which He gave up for us, was a big sacrifice.

The other important thing is the gospel the
priest reads
We can learn from the Readings, to do
our good deeds,
We should sing to our Lord in a great voice
Sing of His glory, praise Him Rejoice.

For our Lord suffered and died on a cross for us all
And our Lord is always with us when we call
So don't go to Mass thinking it's boring, then
sighing
Remember our Lord on the cross when He
was dying.

    P Mason

Dreams

I close my eyes and curl up tight
Pretend the morning still is night.
Oh! How I hate to leave my bed
To face the world and use my head.
When I could lie here, soft and warm
The blankets close around my form.
I drift and dream the time away
And think of what I'd do today.
If I had found the rainbow's end
To make a fortune I could spend.
But blessed freedom's not my lot
Until I find that golden pot.
Beginning of the rainbow's here
But where's the end I am not clear,
Perhaps it is the fact I'm free
To stand and walk, to hear and see.
To count God's blessings and His gifts,
The simple things I know exist.
Throw off the blankets, greet the dawn
And thank you God that I was born.

Clare Astbury

The Stalker

Past now the days of exile, danger, fear,
Days when at every moment death was near;
And David now was king, firm on the throne,
By other nations feared, loved by his own.
No longer constant hardship to endure,
His now the pleasures wealth and power procure.
In all he undertook he knew success:
Affairs of state - and of the heart, no less.
His thoughts went to Bathsheba, and he smiled -
Fairest of women, carrying his child.
True, he had been obliged to plot and scheme
Before she could be brought to his harem;
But he'd succeeded, and no faintest breath
Of scandal linked him with her husband's death.
His plans, his pleasures, none, it seemed, withstood;
David considered life, and found it good.

Nathan approached his king with care that day:
The hunter can become his quarry's prey.
Knowing his first will be his only chance,
The stalker masks his stealthy, slow advance
Till he can aim, and know he will not fail.
Just so did Nathan use his moving tale.
'A wealthy man had flocks and herds and land.
A poor man had one lamb he'd reared by hand,
A child to him, the apple of his eye.
That lamb the rich man seized.' 'The man should die!'
David in righteous anger cried, once more
The shepherd of his flock, as long before.
His quarry David's conscience, Nathan drew
And loosed his bolt: 'That man,' said he, 'is you.'

One stalked his quarry for his own base end;
One that he might, in wounding, heal his friend.

John Lord

A Cross At The Heart Of Love

At the heart of love is a cross,
and there Love died for me;
should I then be afraid of the love
that lies in me?

Satan would ever warn
that I protect myself:
keep closed the heart, don't open up,
for love and pain go hand in hand!

Let Satan's minions flee!
I'll embrace the pain,
not turn my back.
The love in my heart
I won't - I can't deny.
I'll stand firm, be true -
be open and caring,
and risk the pain;
for my Lord is here,
bearing all with me.

If I close the door to shut out the pain
I lose myself, my life, my all:
I shut out my Lord, who is Love Divine.
But, dear Lord God,
do love and happiness for me
never go hand-in-hand?

Am I always doomed only to see and feel
the cross that lies at the heart of love?
It's my privilege, You say,
to share the cross with You -
so be it, Lord, I will step out in love
and share the pain with You!

Diana Wilkinson

The Hem Of His Robe

Here comes Jesus
In scented garments of Lebanon
Light's robe, moving softly, the hem
Over the lands in shade.
Tassels and pomegranates
Bells of silver
Sounding His presence
O High Priest King.

Healing Saviour;
Dew's early light falls the hem of His robe
                              on the earth
Flowing robe
Deep hem
Filling our lives with wholeness
                                 and joy.

Ann Russell

Message To A Young Student On Gaining An Honours Degree

Whatever of talent and skill we possess,
There is the attending by-product of stress,
Whatever great seat of control we attain
That onus of duty upon us is lain.

Then those who have risen to gain others praise,
Are sought out, to speak pearls of wisdom, to amaze,
The higher we rise in the realm of progress,
The harder we fall, if crushed, under duress.

The student who gains learning's highest award,
See pals shift away, feeling envy, or awed.
Life's glories are tarnished by friends who are flawed;
The brightest of moments can sadly, be marred.

If all of our blessings we take as from God,
T'will keep us in Faith, with humility shod.
We never need fall to our doom on the rocks,
Nor ever be ruined by life's heavy knocks.

Created He us for His friendship Divine,
Our hopes and ambitions His love will entwine
If we yield to His Rule and His Sovereign control;
To serve in His Kingdom, this is our true goal.

He'll keep us from slipping down dark shameful roads,
From using our strength for unworthy rewards,
The joy never fading, the peace never lost,
Are ours as we see we are one of the lost,

And then bending low, we reach out to our source,
In heaven-given wisdom, see no other course
But to walk hand in hand with our Heavenly Lord,
The mortal with the Eternal in wondrous accord.

Our greatest achievements, refined by His Grace,
Will give us on earth and in heaven, a place;
Contentment of soul, both in joy and in pain;
The peaks and the troughs of life, never be vain.

The Word of the Lord fulfil all that you do,
Thus, the gift of your friendship will help others through;
Yet, give Him the glory in all you achieve,
T'will be blessed by the measure of how you believe.

Dorothy Wood

The Absence Of Wholeness

Drawing near to your emptiness
I remembered I heard in the Beginning,
The Word.
You have not spoken in secret.
The emptiness is filled with the echo of your voice.
The promised far receding upon the distant hills.
The waters of the Holy One washed upon the shore.
The waves of righteousness ever lapping.
I call to you who dwells in high and holy places,
Your daughter child calls to you,
From the shore of brokeness.
Heed my prayer,
Mend my pain,
Come to me in my desert of emptiness.
Make me whole again.

Sylvia Chambers

Lord Jesus, Your World

Lord Jesus
need we invite you into our world?
This world,
Your world.

Lord Jesus,
what's gone wrong with our beautiful world?
This world,
Your world.

Lord Jesus
can we ever change this sinful world?
This world,
Your world.

Lord Jesus,
take our lives and use them in our world,
for
This world
is
Your world.

Nigel Gotobed

Christ Is The King

O Precious Lord,
There in Your Word,
You said 'Rise up and follow me.'
You made me hear,
And it is clear
I did not choose You, for *You* chose me.
Please take my hand and show me the way,
Oh! Help me Lord, I want to obey,
I'm lost without You, I know it now,
The Love about You, I feel it now.

I knew Your Name,
But to my shame,
Just who You *are*, I did not know.
Then, in a tract,
I learned the fact
I would be Saved by receiving You.
Now in my heart I ask You to stay.
For *You* are *Life,* The *Truth* and The *Way,*
My life is Yours Lord, please take it all,
The Life You gave Lord, You gave for all.

Now every day,
To You I pray
And thank You Lord, You saved my soul,
And so my prayer
Is, I must share
That God is *Real,* and He loves us all.
He owns the world, and we are His own,
You are His Son, the Truth You have shown,
Life after death, Lord, that is no lie.
You conquered death, Lord, and death must die.

There on the Cross,
You burned our dross,
Our every sin You chose to bear.
If we believe
Then we'll receive

New life in You Lord, beyond compare.
'To live is Christ, to die is to gain'
Eternal Joy, where You are to Reign.
Death has no victory, death has no sting.
You are the Victor, *You Are The King*.

Hilda Barrett

God's Back

(Then I will remove my hand, to let you see my back - Exod. 33:23)

Can God be seen?
No one has ever seen God, says John.
No one can ever see him, declares Paul.
What, then, did Moses see on the holy mount?
Was he dazzled by the midday sun
Or blinded by a lightning flash?
God has no form to hide
With outstretched hand while passing by.
What, then, happened to Moses?
Did he feel fear before the elements of nature
And awe at a sensed presence?
Can we accuse the ancient writers
Of objectifying an inner experience,
Of picturing what by its very nature
Cannot be portrayed?
They say that God passed by
As Moses cowered in a cleft of rock
Allowing him to glimpse his back,
The afterglow of his presence.

Let the text stand -
We grasp its import:
Moses encountered God
And his life was changed for ever.

Dennis Tackley

64

Psalm Of Sadness And Depression

Lord, the grey days are outside the window.
Brown-tinted landscape and grey skies merge in the mist;
Darker-grey shapes are pencilled against the horizon
With lombardy poplars I know are there spearing dark grey
towards the sky.
By the pool the dark reeds tangle and the heron waits in vain.
White snow falls and hides everything.

Lord, the greyness outside seeps through into the house;
As Winter is upon us the tears drown my heart
And I long for the brightness to return.
My eyes turn red as the tears spill over;
Life is as miserable as the monochrome outside.
Sadness spears me, as the trees spear the sky.

Lord, stay by my side, my comfort and my Redeemer.

Kathy Warne

Tears

Weep your tears, dear heart
Make no restraint.
Their flow shall water pastures of understanding,
Deep
On whence may feed lives bereft of living
That they may keep
Their sanity.

And Love's return?
Thy very self made free.
The heart shall whisper back
Christ wept for thee.

Joan Russell Sears

Spring's Birth

When icy winds shall cease to blow
With grass emerging from the snow,
And Winter reluctant sloughs her skin
And tentatively Spring moves in.
Early through curtains does sunrise creep
and pierce my eyelids when I'd sleep.
Black-bird swoops and whoops along
With rich and mellow merry song.
Gold star celandine gives birth
Fecund and eager is Mother Earth
Should you ask the way I feel
Ah, Springtime is my Achilles heel
for now shall sap and spirit rise
the surge of love becomes a Paradise
And do the primroses still grow
On Speeton cliffs as long ago?

Barbara Robson

Our Father

Our Father who art in Heaven, hallowed by Thy name.
How often we recite these words, but still we are to blame
For treating God with disrespect, we hang our heads with shame,
And yet we sin.
Thy kingdom come, Thy will be done, that means right here on
earth.
But do we ever stop to think, how much those words are worth.
Or even contemplate, the reason for Christ's birth.
How can God win?
He overlooks our trespasses, and gives our daily bread,
But do we truly thank the Lord in prayers sincerely said.
Or do we take it as our right, and look away instead.
Our lives to live.
Temptation is a thing of choice, he would not lead us there
We're tempted of our own freewill
But God is well aware
That power and glory overcome when we are in despair.
God will forgive.

Juliet C Eaton

Grey

Where do you go when you feel trapped and imprisoned?
How do you grasp beauty in creation?
How do you find the colours again when all looks grey?
Where do you go when night is day?
The outline of the trees look bleak against the sky line
No sign of Spring . . . .
The fog obliterates the sun and horizon
No sign of Spring . . . .
Are there no bulbs under the frost?
Are there no bulbs appearing through the soil?
No sign of Spring. No sign of life. No hope to go on.
But Jesus came to give us hope. He alone tells me to go on. He alone
Will change the darkness into light.
I will trust you Lord because I know the Spring will always come.

Angie Quinnell

Obedience

Ideas aplenty come tumbling through
My brain that's alert, with initiative too.
'I'll take her some flowers, or maybe a cake,
I'm sure she'd appreciate something I bake.

Perhaps 'twould be better if I were to offer,
On Thursday this week to baby-sit for her.
She'd really enjoy getting out for a treat,
Without all the little ones under her feet.

Or, there's a thought, I'll make her a sweater
That will keep her warm in this wintry weather.
Pink, purple and black are colours she'd suit,
And just for a treat, mohair would look good.

Another idea's to give her an invite,
To lunch on a Sunday would be a delight.
She'd not have to cook, or clean up the mess,
Just sit and enjoy without hurry and stress.'

But then all at once I stop in my tracks.
This might be all right, but sadly it lacks
That inner conviction that comes from above,
On bringing our friend to the One whom we love.

When I saw her in need, before I began
To jiggle and juggle with all that I plan,
I should have remembered it really is worth
Some quiet with God before spouting forth.

He knows her far better, and what she is needing.
Some prayer for a start, real, true interceding
That those whom she loves would come and be blest,
By the One whom she serves and knows is the best.

It would take time and effort, this business of prayer,
Action's my thing, not kneeling somewhere.
But then there's the joy, the praise and the pleasure
Of knowing it happened through me in a measure.

If they came to Christ, it wouldn't be long
Before all around sense her smile and her song.
I'm sure she'd have liked anything that I gave,
But revelled far more in His power to save.

So next time I'm ready to help one in need,
I'll try and remember God's face to seek.
And maybe, who knows, next time it might be,
That what is required is a cake baked by me!

Marian Whitaker

Challenge

Behold
When I stand at the door
and knock - shall I see
on the day I arrive
it's alive?

Peace - be still
My Word to seven churches
receive, if you will.
He that hath ears to hear
Let him hear.

Tell me now,
if I am your first love.
Are you faithful? and how?
Hot or cold? - I will scorn
the lukewarm.

I will search
for my own, so hold fast
'til I come, Build my Church
If you build it on prayer -
I'll be there.

D J Robinson

The Forget Me Not

Blue for the mantle of Mary
Blue for the evening sky.
Blue for the flower in the garden
On whose petals the raindrops glisten
Like sapphires sparkling there.

She decorates the garden and pathways
You'll find her in woodland and vale
By the high grass and the rambling Rose,
Near the tall trees whose leaves dance with
the breeze.
By the good and gracious fields
Where the rain falls soft and clear.

One remembers the little Flower of Carmel
who never her monastery left
Yet travelled to the ends of the earth
On the jewels of her trusting prayer.
Down through the ages of time.
Childlike haunts of our Lady's children
Gather garlands and fragrant blossoms rare,
To greet you O Mary Beloved Lady
Joy of the Holy Trinity, lady of Bethlehem.
Hear us then most gentle Mother
And forget not one prayer
Till in the Garden of Delight
Neath thy mantle - all thy children
One day shall shine.
Blue for the mantle of Mary. Blue for the evening sky.
Blue for the flower in the garden. On whose petals the
Raindrops glisten, like sapphires sparkling there.

Kathy Barry

Untitled

Clouds of darkness roll across the night sky,
thunder rumbles across the heavens,
and the daylight beckons
sunrise glorious in magnificence
heralds a new beginning, a new day,
a new awakening.
The light will always return
quenching out the darkness
and Jesus will always have the victory.
You may yet to go through battle
but the war has already been won.
Jesus is victorious
even now prepares for his return.
So awaken you sleeping people
slumber no longer
in dingy, dark corners
the light will find you
Jesus is waiting!

Delia Jane Morritt

A Factory Worker's Prayer

Christ of the common way! We did not ask
To sit on sunlit hills of Galilee
And listen to Your Voice; it is our task
To toil amid the noise of industry.
But this we pray; open our ears and eyes
To hear Your Voice in every turning wheel,
To see Your footprints on a dusty floor
And in our fellow-workers lives to feel
Your moving spirit, Lord; we ask no more -
Christ of our working day.

Mary Hunt

To Mary On Calvary

Pale wood I kneel before,
Carved by believer's hand
Into the image of your dying Son,
Carved in love and care.

Stretched torn and naked
On a cross of death
By cruel and callous soldiers,
In the cause of hate,
The body of your Son
You gazed upon in unbelief.

Mary, Mother, his and mine,
In your mind then
Did the question rise,
'Why me?'
Was this the moment when you said,
'Is this the answer to my
'How can it be'?'

Torn and bleeding
  bruised and pierced,
Flesh of your flesh,
  blood of your blood.

Yet
Your Son's death you
  from sin
    did save,
That he
  from you
    might
Pure untainted life
  attain,
And sinless
  become sin,

To save
        a sinful race.

Pale polished wood
        is not
Your Son in agony.

Lead me, Mary,
        to the body
Of that Son
        stretched suffering
Upon the cross
        of this world
Today.

There Jesus dies
Where mother cradles dying child
Against her flat and milkless breasts.

There Mary helpless weeps
Where poverty sows seeds of pain
And reaps a harvest of death.

When Christian Christian fights and kills in hate,
Then Jesus' head once more with thorns is crowned.

Then Mary silent weeps to see Christ die,
When people call others less than them,
For being black,
        or white,
                or different.

With cruel whips the flesh of Christ is torn,
Whenever I turn in upon myself the love
I owe to others,
        and use them,
Not honouring:
'Whate'er you do to the least of these
                you do to me.'

Mary, Mother, his and mine,
                    teach me
That there must I
                    your Jesus find,
Wherever people live
                    and die
                              in misery.

Patrick J Sharpe M S C

Silver Wedding

The wind blows.
Trees sway and leaves swirl
away, gone forever.
Husbands part, or wives,
following the wind's desire,
forbidden fruit calls
and men fall,
the children cry.
Half of all marriages break down,
break hearts, break a nation.
Half of all marriages hurt, and choose
the easy route
(but not for the children).
Half of all marriages are no more,
except for the children.

But half of all marriages stay,
they don't betray
the trust of a friend
but work on through to a
sweeter end.
Hearts are caught and
chords not cut,
tempests come but they
don't tip the boat.
The journey is made together,
blown by the breath of God
and families that face the weather
grow with each other
and honour the Lord.

Jane Upchurch

In Your Arms (Mark 10:16)

In your arms I know your
awesome strength around me;
In your arms I know you're
holding me so tight.
In your arms I know your
Fatherly protection,
You're the one who's with me
every day and night.

In your arms I know there'll
always be forgiveness,
In your arms I know I can't
put up a fight;
In your arms I know I long
to be still closer,
You're the one who's changed
my darkness into light.

In your arms I know your
constant affirmation,
In your arms I know I'm
precious in your sight;
In your arms I know the
love you pour upon me,
You're the one in whom I can
have true delight.

In your arms I know the
ultimate contentment,
In your arms I know your
Majesty and might;
In your arms I know I've
seen a glimpse of heaven,

In your arms I know that
everything's alright, Lord;
In your arms I know that
everything's alright.

Malcolm Hill

The Beginning And The End

Lord God Almighty,
You are the beginning
and the end.
In You
and with You alone,
everything that was,
that is,
that ever will be,
began.

You see in an instant
both the start and the finish.
You hold them in Yourself,
in Your very being.

The span of the ages
is as a moment to You.
How marvellous then
that You should also see
the minute details
of our fragmented lives,
of each earthly hour that passes -
even each second -
and care to enter into them.

This then, is the miracle -
the wonder of Your inconceivable greatness
stooping to enter
our earthbound smallness,
and by Your entry
transforming the finite to infinite,
and drawing humanity
towards eternity.

Catherine Aldis

Memories Of Fading Green

I have memories of green beyond you,
green and a river, it was
Cambridge, punting. Us, drunk,
while our mutual friend steered.
We laughed, in the green,
under the whisper of breezed trees
among the lap of cool water
How I loved you then,
I love you still.
But you have gone on, you
might as well be dead, you do not
exist in my world.
You died late last night
after soft farewells, you died;
faded out in the autumn street.
I think you are fading in my head now,
you aren't as clear as before,
only the occasional image;
laughing outside a pub in Camden
last summer. We loved so deeply.
Yet you come clearer fewer days.
I miss you still after all that's happened,
how many months have died away?
Yet I have memories of fading green,
and of bluer skies and softer breezes
and of you, laughing in the summer,
and me loving you. So much.

Anne Marie O'Callaghan

Renewal Faith

Out of the darkness there comes light
A cloud of butterflies alight
Coloured wings of gossamer down
How they flutter and hover around
Sweet scented flower attracting them anew
Welcoming sun rain shadow and you
God's wealth of happiness will abound
when such as you turn around

Amen

J M Ford

Prayer For My Son

What was good enough for me
when I was young
is another world to him.

If I push him into a mould
I must expect to see the cracks,
if I trap him like a butterfly,
he may never learn to fly.

I'll give him freedom to stretch his wings
and fly to seek his destiny;
then, if he falls, I'll give him love
to mend his wings,
and encouragement to start again,
however many times.

I'll watch his flight through sun and showers
with my prayers beneath his wings.

Mary Care

A Prophet's Prayer

O Lord of my heart
to Thee do I come
when shadows fall
and the light grows dim,
helplessly burdened with
sorrow and sin,
O Lord of my heart
to Thee do I come.

O Lord of my heart
to Thee do I come
with gladness, humbly
accepting forgiveness and
mercy.
In spirit and truth
to love and to worship,
O Lord of my heart
to Thee do I come.
                    Amen

Susan J Rchardson

Morning Thoughts

Creeping downstairs, in slippered feet,
Pulling back curtains, a new day to greet,
Putting on the kettle, setting plates and cups,
I love this time of day, when I'm first up,
The family still asleep upstairs,
I gather strength for all the chores,
Pleasures, duties, the new day brings,
Outside the world awakens, stretches and yawns,
Many sleepy eyes open to greet the morn,
Outside, streets awaken to familiar sounds,
Milkman, Postman, Paper boy on their rounds,
These are the simple things of everyday life,
While all I ask, in my home, my loved one's
Peace of mind and strength to face the day.

W G Whalley

Far Removed Parents

Being an only child is not much fun
Especially when mother and father won't play when work is done
They tell me to amuse myself I totally disagree
And insist upon some one to keep me company
Mother and father have no time for their one and only child
You would think that being alone that child would grow wild
No completely different as well mannered this child turned out to be
Self disciplined an attractive all under control but so lonely

Mother is off to one of her meetings she is the president of this and
                                                                    that
Father a banking official known usually as the aristocrat
They employ a cook and a cleaning lady who are lots of fun
The lonely child enjoys their company especially when school is done
Such tales and wonderment do these three share alone in that big
                                                                    house
While cook prepares some delicacies the cleaning lady spies a mouse
Don't be scared the lonely child whispers as it is caught in a trap
Release it in the garden dear be careful of the cat

What a scrumptious meal cook does provide both mother and father
                                                                    agree
She deserves a higher wage so poor her rate of pay this the lonely
                                                    child remarks temptingly
Also the cleaning lady who is so conscientious and never makes a
                                                                    fuss
Father says he will think about this and he does sure enough
Their wages have been increased and all harmony restored
Mother and father now satisfied also their one adored
It has been suggested that the lonely child to a boarding school next
                                                                    term
Will this upset the household? As the lonely child must learn

  R D Hiscoke

88

Echoes

Echoes of silence resounded through depths of despair
Wandering through aeons of space knowing he does not care
Silence that fills me was once just an echoing roar
Silence engulfs me where once I could hear eagles soar

Echoes of silence consume all my night and my day
A cavernous void of despair keeps my anger at bay
Silence inside me destroys all the sounds that I love
And a screeching seagull which mimics the sound of a dove

Echoes of silence compound as I lay on my bed
As love turns to hate with all these tears I have shed
Echoes of laughter receded as silence invades
The dream is for real as reality silently fades

Echoes of silence resounded through depths of despair
The sound of his voice which beckoned me into his lair
Silence still fills me with sorrow and sonorous roar
But now it is golden with sound and the man I adore.

Judy Studd

The Cemetery

I was walking through the cemetery, one dark and windy night.
When I heard this tapping. God it gave me such a fright.
It was coming from this new grave stone, that was very clear.
I went over to investigate. I was real nervous as I got near.
I peered over the grave stone. The man had a chisel in his hand.
He was knelt chipping at the grave stone. The chippings were as
                                                                                               sand.
Why are you working here at midnight. I asked in a casual way.
I got no answer. I said couldn't you carry out the work by day.
The man paused and looked up. A strange glint was in his eyes.
They spelt my bleeding name wrong. Was then that I realised.
It was a ghost that I was talking to. I had shivers up my back.
With that he got up and walked away. His tools in a hessian sack.

Don Goodwin

Go With The Flow

Today, as I entered my living room,
I was happy, in both mind and heart.
But, before I departed, I left there in gloom,
Two choices drove me apart.
'Go with the flow' suggests Stuart
'Your courage will take you to the end.'
'Your pen will describe your journey'
Says God my leader and friend.

Like Solomon, I need to apply wisdom,
I'm now flowing the two side by side.
With my pen held aloft as I float downstream,
I'm hoping and praying, it's all just a dream.
And I'm reaching the end of the tide.
I've reached the end of life's journey.
There were times I rebelled against rules,
But experience taught me that to go with the flow,
Was much easier, than to argue with fools.

I'm older and wiser, sifting musk from the grain.
Accepting friends who are faithful and true.
I now go with the flow, and flow as I write.
I acknowledge both points of view.

William Price

Penrith

From high on the hill I look down;
There below me lies our town.
This town called Penrith is my home;
From this lovely place I will not roam.

It gives me pleasure and delight
To see it from this great height,
Looking down on the houses and streets
Where people walk and they meet.

The castle and station catch my eye
As through the station a train goes by.
I watch the train travelling so fast,
Then on the fells my eyes are cast.

Away in the distance these fells lie;
They seem to reach up to the sky,
And as the sun beams down on them,
These Lakeland mountains are a gem.

As I sit and watch over our town
I think of the good times which abound.
We'll stay here in this town until we die;
We love this place, my wife and I.

Francis Allen

King Of Heaven

The Lord God in Heaven, watches over us all each night.
He pulls us through the darkness, till the early morning light.
He brings us all joy, when we feel all alone.
From his kingdom above, he watches over our homes.

He listens intently, to all the words we say.
He gives you comfort, when your down each day.
He soothes your aching heart, that's filled with pain.
He forgives all sins, and gives you his love again.

He's always by your side, whenever there's a need.
His love is for free, in a world filled with greed.
No charges for his forgiveness, as you pray to him each night.
He is the King of Heaven, a star that shines so bright.

Ask and you will receive, the good book tells us all.
No matter what it is, no task is too small.
If you believe in him, his love will keep you warm.
A soldier of the Lord, never comes to any harm.

Give him your love, God who reigns in Heaven above.
He will give you a heart, that overflows with love.
He awaits you in Heaven, his Kingdom way up high.
All your sorrows will disappear, no more will you cry.

Kevin P Collins

The Desert

Tonight the desert is cold, in stark contrast to the burning heat of the
day.
I shiver, and clasp my blanket tighter around me.
All about me is sand - not the smiling sand of the seashore
with children playing happily -
but uninviting and potentially cruel.
Suddenly, in the dark mantle of the sky, a star blazes forth,
And lights a small flicker of hope within my breast.
With hope in my heart I sleep - and dream of trees growing by
a gurgling stream.
Running water, living water.
I remember the words of Jesus,
'Out of the believer's heart shall flow rivers of Living Water.'
Lord, let your living water flow into me, and through me onto others;
Let me be a window through which your light can shine,
To lead others to the oasis where Living Water springs forth,
To cleanse, strengthen, heal and renew.
Dawn breaks, and I see the desert with different eyes.
A place of solitude and peace;
Of beauty and of calm.
I return from whence I came,
Knowing that the desert can be both dangerous and a safe haven;
A place of fearsome sounds, yet full of peace.
A place where I can meet with God and let His love pour into
me and through me.
A place to be alone with God,
But also to learn to meet others in fellowship, as brothers
and sisters in Christ.

Elaine Brockelbank

Moss-Shadowed Steps

These steps would glide beneath her thoughts of plenty
Thoughts of all night dances
Evening walks beside a moonlit sea
Foxtrot and quickstep
The key in her slender hand quick and easy
Turning the lock and ticking clock
Enters her world of welcome and sound
But now she is old and closer to the ground
She falters and looks up and round
Her eyes bright and roaming
Her youth comes running
Laughing at herself
Speaks of a photograph on the kitchen shelf
Thinks of a kiss
Climbs those moss-shadowed steps
And makes a wish.

Paul Andrew Jones

Be Happy

Be happy not sad,
Don't cry be glad.
Don't moan or groan,
Just give or loan.
Don't frown or shout,
Be glad let it out,
Don't be angry or down,
Lift your head and wear a crown.
Don't swear or curse,
Just give, reimburse.
Don't kick or scream,
Relax have a dream.
Don't abuse or mock,
Times short look at the clock.
Don't harass or molest,
Do your best,
Don't be a vandal and cause strife,
Remember God gave us the wonder of life.

Beryl Welch

The Light Is Coming

Four tall candles
Each a different
Hue . . . .
Bright Advent
Colours,
Mauve and Pink,
And White
And Blue . . . .
Adorn the
Season's
Altar . . . .
For the Coming of
The Light!
. . . .The change from
Darkness!
Winter's garb!
Renewing Life
With
New born
Advent
Dawn! . . . .
Each new Light
Preparing
Week by week
The Faithful
For the
Coming of
The Lord! . . . .

Wm Paul McDermott

On The Road

I'm on the road to somewhere
With sweet Jesus by my side.
I'm tired of going nowhere
Looking for a place to hide.

I've found a sense of purpose
To replace the emptiness.
Where once I was benighted,
By the light I have been blessed.

I am leaving sterile desert
Searching for a promised land,
A travel guide companion
Is the Bible in my hand.

J G Ryder

Queen Of The May

The sighting of the first snowdrop and crocuses
All these pretty flowers brighten the days for us
The gardens and hedge grows are ablaze with colour
And seeing the beauty of these flowers can be yours

A bit later come the flood of the golden daffodils
The daffodils grow in the valleys and on the hills
The gardens are ablaze with golden glory
On round abouts, on greens and could make up a story

At Easter's time they meet the needs of all celebrations
A bunch of pretty flowers given to anyone of special occasions
Carnations, roses, lilies, hydrangea and sunflowers
These flowers have sweet and scenting powers

Mounting roses with their red and very big heads
And the smaller flowers made up for newly weds
Then the little flowers put in baskets in May is a way
Of offering up to Mary of the Queen of the May

R T Owen

Alcudia Meeting

Searing hot, Spanish Sun on golden stone,
The church stood out in majestic glory.
Through a door, within a door,
To a lofty cool interior, where . . . .
Prismatic hues of welcome light,
Danced away from the ancient glass.
We two were alone, completely, there,
Silent, relaxed,
To marvel, to kneel and humbly pray.
Often, at Mass, I've prayed, but,
Here was peace,
Wonderful, strengthening, calming peace.
Beyond understanding, uplifting the soul.
God was there and near to his throne.
Intense communion, over too soon,
The Church door opened and
The World
Moved
In.

Wilf Woolley

Winter's Gown

Winter arrives in crisp white cape
Of wispy wedding lace,
As feather snowflakes flutter down
And brush against her face.
Icicles like glistening gems
Are sparkling in the light,
As Mother Nature spreads around
A beauty clear and bright.
Leafless trees with empty boughs
Are bathed in rosy glow
As silent earth lies fast asleep
Beneath the mantling snow.

Angela George

A Winter Scene

Winter is here - it snowed last night
Covering the ground in a blanket of white
The air is hushed with muffled sound
A lonely grass tip peeps up from the ground
Patterns of lace on the windowpane
Jack Frost's effort has not been in vain
Snow laden branches diamond bright
A mystical, magical, fairyland sight
A happy snowman has appeared in the park
With button nose and coal eyes dark
A bright red scarf, pipe of clay
He looks so grand on this wintry day
Mischievous children shriek with delight
Deeply engrossed in a snowball fight
Over the rise more sport has begun
To pepper their day with frivolous fun
A young lad on toboggan off and away
Whilst his pal makes do with his mother's tin tray
Fragile and small in the flower bed
A brave little snowdrop raises her head
This delicate flower has pushed through the earth
There to remind us of nature's re-birth
A soft snowy silence, a wondrous sight
When the earth is cloaked in a raiment of white.

Barbara Davies

Christmas Fairy

I wonder what it's like to be
The Fairy on the Christmas tree.
Looking down from lofty height
A vantage point for watching life.
They've only got twelve days to preen
They all must feel just like a queen.
Though the other toys could be a pain
Falling off and getting crushed
Causing such a dreadful fuss.
Sometimes that must make them blush.

Stability's what it's all about
Holding on tight and lasting out.
It's not that long when you work it out.
And giving pleasure must be such fun
High pitched screams of pure delight
Little flushed faces by candlelight.
I wonder, do they appreciate the fuss
And it must be annoying all that dust.
Then all boxed up with love and care
They're off to sleep until next year.

Brenda Norman

God's Gift

Thou I have eyes to see,
And ears to listen too.
To see the day, and hear it say,
A big hello to you.
You can smell the early morn,
That sound, of just a day.
How can you count the many things,
That's put there, in your way.
The feeling deep inside you
Your heart, it wants to burst,
Your wishing every single thing,
That you! Had seen it first.
You know it's always been there,
You just needed time to look.
Oh what a gift for God to give
It's nature's open book.

Dorothy Marshall Bowen

The Lord's Gifts

The Lord God gave us eyes to see
The beauty all around.
He gave us ears to hear with
To listen to the sounds.
He gave a voice to talk with
And to some a voice to sing
To bring to us the melodies
And hear the church bells ring.
He gave a nose to smell the fragrance in the air,
The smell of mixed aromas
That all of us can share.
Hands to tend his garden
And watch the flowers grow,
From the different plants and seed
He gave to us to sow.
He gave us limbs to walk with
And limbs to build our homes,
He gave us hearts to love with
And to care for those alone.
All these gifts we treasure
But the greatest gift of all,
Is the gift of life itself,
He gives to one and all.

P Ratcliffe

Gifts From God

So many gifts God gave me, just look around and see,
Good and loving parents, this feeling, that I'm free.
The sunrise and the sunset, the moon to see at night,
The mountains and the rivers, such a glorious sight.

All the trees and flowers, and all the smells so sweet,
Good company; and a decent place to sleep.
A husband who is gone now, and children, there were four,
A place to live; with my very own front door.

And the neighbours cat, she likes to come and call,
Then precious time; to spend, with one and all.
Vegetables in the garden, grown by a loving son,
I guess I'm really lucky, when all is said and done.

For I have so many good gifts, sent from up above,
The love that I can really feel, is sent to me,
                        by God.

Barbara Callaghan

Count Your Blessings

When you've troubles on your mind,
When your heart is sad,
When you feel no-one is kind
And everything seems bad,
Then look around and everywhere
You will see God's gifts are there.

Birds a'singing in the trees,
Flowers dancing in the breeze,
Wispy clouds just passing by
In the heavens way up high,
Sights and sounds for all to share,
Gifts from God are everywhere.

V Holden

Past Shades And Shadows

Brum is the large city where I was born,
In a bleak room not quite a flat,
At the darkest hour before the dawn.
None of which was a welcome mat!

My parents had married two months before,
Duty bound because I was there.
I was hardly the one they could adore,
I made their joys in life more rare.

With them poverty took its toll too much,
And sapped the recent vows they made.
It took away their one remaining crutch,
A foolish pride to make the grade.

When winter goes and brighter summer comes
It should bring Nature's love in fruits,
But in the cities rich from many slums
Are those forgetful of their roots.

To Gran's we moved when I was barely three,
To me I knew she was not kind.
She lived alone in black, and could not see,
But most folk too were often blind.

My face she traced 'He is ugly' she said,
I felt so hurt but understood,
For on the days she was ill in bed
It was I that was feeling good!

After she died she came to me at night,
Her face at peace with saintly smile.
She was so young, and ghostly garbed in white,
A loving angel in her style.

She did not speak, but I knew she loved me,
My vibrations were in rapport.
Since then she's been my sacred tree,
And guide to summer's fruit galore!

B Garradley

Going To Be

We are going to be married
What ever you say
Because we wish to be together
Every single day.

We are going to be married
Even if you do not come
For we intend to have years together
And in God's eyes live together as one.

We are going to be married
Yes it is all arranged
Why do you look so shocked
Did you think I would always stay the same.

We are going to be married
Though it is not what you want
But try and be happy for us dad
And along with God enjoy the moment.

Keith L Powell

A Walk Through The Forest

I can sense that you're there Lord,
I can sense that you're there,
In the fragrance of the pine-trees,
And the crispness of the air.

The people walking arm in arm,
The colour of the sky.

The way the sun rests softly,
On the branches of the tree,
It warms my heart to you Oh Lord,
And brings a smile to me.

Again you're in a blade of grass,
In the statement that it makes,
And in the flight of ducks and birds,
Across the ripples of the lakes.

David Sawyer

Gifts From God: The Beloved

Is not a place where quails skirt their way
and white jumpers grow, holy?
Is not a place where lives touch and hope stirs, holy?
Is not this, his place where bread was shared, wine blessed
and love born, his dwelling?

His life wove a web of glory,
Its threads drew him to One Who:
Catches the sun in stillness, holds a wind's rush
and sees with more than sight;
Traps a radiance in the hive's crush,
and knows the singleness of all that is;
Fingers dew, dyes dawn's flush,
And images truth in us.

He said, 'Love lies on our hearts as the sign of who we are.
It draws us to serve each other to the end.
It is the truth of each life,
Knitting together as lover and beloved.'

Now he stands on a shore which no chart can fix,
and watches the shearwaters glide to the sea's edge.
Now he hears melodies which no voice can make
and greets his Beloved.
So, stippled with glory, he puts on a sun's splendour,
and is encompassed by Love.

D H Webster

God's Glorious Gift - One Countless Host

Abram, Isaac, Jacob nomads,
Knew God in events as granddads.
Like unseen seed making harvests,
Rooted in land, fed by tempests.
In silence God's voice called Moses,
To free slaves from Egypt's clutches.

Seekers meet Christ in history,
Four friends lift roof, no mystery.
Paralytic healed by Jesus,
Wrongs reconciled with skill wondrous.
God appears when Truth is tried out,
Purified friend, transformed drop-out.

Our world spends millions on missiles,
Heedless of starving juveniles.
Today widespread conflict on earth,
Where some thousands are brought to birth.
Crimes of men obscure life's vision.
God through faith brings renovation.

Our blest eternal lineage,
Leads us to Heaven's harbourage,
Christ's kingly rule knows no defeat,
In us His reign of grace complete.
Liberate rebel hearts from greed,
Willing helping hands reach all need.

Heirs of the Spirit's liberty,
Kindled with generosity,
At work throughout the world today;
In strength that none can take away.
God's great gift - His glorious goal,
Countless hosts with one Oversoul.

James Leonard Clough

Gifts From God

If I were to write my gifts from God
a page would never do
I now know all the pain I've had
his arms were around me too

We take for granted every day
things - that happen in the past
To thank him for life itself
understanding the pain won't last

To thank him for three healthy girls
for the husband that I had
To realise only now
that happy can mean sad

My mother, father, sisters too
such precious people, always true
Nephew, nieces, grandchildren love
these are all gifts from above

My prayers seem longer as years go by
so many things that underlie
His reasons for the lives we've had
not even knowing it wasn't so bad

Dear God the very thought of it
now remains to see
I did not know I was happy then
I have to let that be

Age alone a learning game
values change, they're not the same
I now can thank him for nearly dying
I lost my way, he was crying

Mistakes I've made were not in vain
only causing grief and pain
to myself a hundredfold
to make amends by being told

To thank God for all his gifts
my dogs, friends, my spirits lift
Giving love, helping others
god kept me here - just another . . . .

Jean Tennent Mitchell

Gifts From God

Snowdrops and crocus in early spring,
Glorious weather that summer can bring,
The moon riding high in a cloudy night,
Stars in the heavens twinkling bright.

Sand on the shore caressed by the sea,
The beauties of nature for all to see,
The birds and the bees, flowers and trees,
Cats, dogs, other pets are sure to please.

The rainbow after a thunderstorm,
A fire in winter to keep you warm,
Autumn leaves that are turning to gold,
Ice and snow making your fingers cold.

Travelling along life's busy road,
Helping a friend, sharing a load,
Meeting together to praise the Lord,
Learning more about the Son of God.

The love of family, and of friends,
The love of God that never ends,
The promises found in His holy word,
All of these are the Gifts from God.

W C Niel

An Unknown Pathway

When twilight embraces the cool of the day
And strands of moonlight around me play,
The shadows and memories crowd into my mind
The hopes and the dreams I've left behind.
An unknown pathway, what lies before,
What mysteries for me, from God's treasure store?
New riches, new dreams, new hopes I see
In a world of beauty - so precious to me.
If I hold the moments like a silken thread
By God's divine grace I'll be safely led,
Into a future that will always shine
Where a loving God rests His hands on mine.

Jean Mackenzie

A Gift From God

Skin so soft, eyes so blue
A new born babe from God to you,
Flowers growing with blooms so bright
The sun shining down, the moon beam at night
The morning bird song, a pure white dove
Seem to be gifts from God up above
Spring lambs a jumping in meadows so green
Mountains so high the peak can't be seen
the horizon over the ocean so blue
the pleasure of watching it slip from view
Swans with their cygnets swimming in style
the ducks butting in once and a while
the rabbits bobbing about in the Park
the harmony heard from the song of a lark
all these things are gifts from God for all of us to see
no charge is asked no ticket to buy all absolutely free
but the best gift of all if your blessed, is the birth of
                            your child so divine
a true gift I'd say, every mother's best day
at least I know it was mine
So say thanks now and then like I do, for those nice things
                            to see
A gift from God, yes I think so, sent with love for you and
                            for me.

C Freeman

118

Reflections

The motion of the water stirs my face
Ripple upon ripple, in it's place
Each one reaching for the nearest shore
Equidistant to the one before
Reflection in the water, who am I?
This image looking upward towards the sky
Is your liquid vision keener than my own
Or can it simply all be shattered with a stone
You look deep into my heart and know my thoughts -
There are many ripples there that life distorts
Though gazing back at you I see my soul
Reflected in your image is my goal
I dip my hand into your fluid form
The movement of my fingers soft and warm
You shudder with the shock and then disperse
Reaching out to every corner of the universe.

Phillippa Benson

Whispers Of Eternity

When 'earthly' things are not enough and *your* obvious need battles with *my* inner 'being' though kept under wraps, *passion* personified in the 'spirit' of the moment, soaring above time, elements and earthly things,
stronger even than physical 'oneness', enveloping and encompassing the senses totally in unison.

We come together through lifetimes, reliving our past journeys 'experiencing' extreme tenderness in *this*, holding the dream towards infinity, towards an eager tomorrow, growing and feeling unspoken thoughts but *all* woven by the same thread of constancy.

This universal *surge* of energy soaring together through all time and spheres sharing, forever these 'whispers of eternity'. . . . .

Elaine Edgar

Gifts From God

Oh Father in your wisdom,
You showed me the way,
There is a time for sorrow,
There is a time to pray.

And in your great wisdom,
You chose a path for me,
One which I will follow Lord,
And loyal I will be.

You sent your son down to this earth,
To teach us right from wrong,
Then you took him back again,
Knowing we'd go along.

I try to follow your teaching Lord,
Sometimes I fall away,
But then I hear your gentle voice,
Turn back my son you say.

So sometimes if I'm wrong my Lord,
I know you'll put me right,
When you walk beside me Lord,
I know I'll win the fight.

Cyril Maunders

Christ's Rising My Hope

Christ be my guide as I follow Thy way,
Thy words in my heart, Thy voice by my side.
Christ give me strength to take up my cross.
Thy life in my thoughts, Thy light in my day,
Thy passion to guard me and keep me from pride,
Thy rising my hope, redeeming my loss.

Christ be my master in action this day,
Thy voice in the silence, Thy rule in my life.
Christ be within me; Christ be around me
In all that I do, in all that I say,
Thy love in my joy, thy strength in my strife,
Thy spirit to bless me in all that I see.

Christ be my hope at the hour of my death,
Thy love as my guard, thy mercy my light.
Christ bring me calm in the face of my fear,
Thy glory around me, thy prayer on my breath,
Thy presence my peace, Thy face in my sight.
In life and in death, let Thine be the word that I bear.

Uvedale Tristram

The Path

The one set of footsteps is
All I see as it seems I've
Been carried on his back
For a lifetime: Each pace
Designed with meticulous
Detail so that I never feel . . . .

Alone.
Destiny, Fate, luck has many aliases
But there is only one divine power
Who has moulded and created
The me that is of today.

Pushed along by the gentle
Wind of the pre-ordained
Decisions are no longer
My own to make
I simply mutter humble
Communication and the response
Is quick and clear.

Why worry when my life
Is not my own?
Surely it is divine will
That reigns supreme?

We are very good
At cutting our own messy paths
Not with the same precision
Taking ill-advised diversions.

I hope life has taught me
Out of arrogant decisions
And I've learned to let go of
The control - that ultimately
Belongs to one much wiser
And skilled than I.

Tola Ositelu

The Gift Of Tears

The dewdrops of my tears
Fall sweetly down my face,
Gently wetting my skin
With the tenderness of soft summer rain.

The tears rise up
From a warmth and sadness
Deep within my soul.

They are not truly mine -
I don't control their birth.
It is a higher power than I
Which brings these warm and powerful tears to life.

They are a gift,
And in their falling,
As the soft summer rain
Gives life to new shoots from the ground,
So from these healing tears
New life will spring in me.

Pat Marsh

The Wonders Of The World

Bird, butterfly or flower the sight of them makes my heart pound,
How I love that singing bird's sound,
The taking time from it's business to rest on the ground,
There's so much beauty if you look around,
Here's hoping nature's wonders will always abound.

Ann Woolven

Intimations

*'Daughter, give up praying many beads, and
think such thoughts, as I shall put into your mind.'*
The Book of Marjery Kempe Ch 5

'This creature' she said, knowing herself dot small,
One among multitudes walking the earth, yet all
Graciously loved without knowing how or why. I turned
With her to see a rail-track's wintry wreckage
Fractured by unspoiled sunlight; a spring of blunt
Berries, cracked rubble, smeared with rancid leafage,
As if disfigurement of tarnished man and stone
Alike were grasped, washed clean as wool, accepted.

The Metro train sped on. Alongside ours I saw
Her distanced age, both equally impoverished,
And yet baptised by the sun's open blessing.
Passengers crowding in at each new station glowed
As if when she said, 'It's full merry in heaven'
They'd intimations of it, earthed in them, unploughed.

   Alan C Brown

Child

'What colour is the wind?' she asked.
And again,
'What colour is the wind?'
She was five years old:
Where to begin?
Another question.

I looked into her face.
'Grey, grey like your great eyes.'
'No!' She answered.
'No! When the wind blows the clouds are black.'
'Then it is black, like your long plait.'
No, she would not have it.

'It must be all colours,' said she.
'Then close your eyes,' said I,
'And think of all the colours in the rainbow
Stitched together, like a quilt.
Now, when God shakes it, winds will blow,
All colours . . .'

. . . She was fast asleep.

Dennis Thorogood

Communion Hymn

Come meet beneath the Cross,
To bring our Lord to mind,
And celebrate His saving love
For us and all mankind.

Then gather by the tomb,
To learn He is not there,
Raised by the power of God to live
In triumph everywhere.

Recline around the board,
For fellowship divine,
With Jesus Christ our living Lord,
In broken bread and wine.

In this brief resting place,
We make our spirits' home,
Proclaim the Gospel of His grace,
Until the Saviour come.

We'll meet Him in the air,
Or rise up from the grave,
To join with those who have gone before,
The ones He came to save.

Forever round the throne,
We'll then adore His Name,
And eat with all His ransomed folk,
The supper of the Lamb.

So celebrate the feast,
Rejoice in sins forgiven,
Exult in Jesus' present love,
And taste the joys of Heaven.

Fred Stainthorpe

God Is Love

We all have gifts of one kind or another
And these range from great to small;
We are told we take after our father or mother,
But God's love for us is the greatest of all.

It is deeper and wider than anything known
And is given freely to all;
There are no conditions, it is not on loan,
And so beautiful, it cannot ever pall.

This unstinted love can be seen in the eyes
Of our children, or a faithful pet,
For they put their trust in and idolise
We who love them without hindrance or let.

And we must love God in that same childlike way
For He's our Father in Heaven above.
He sent us Jesus, the ultimate sacrifice to pay.
We can truly say 'no man hath greater love'.

Marlene Allen

God's Gift

Have you just found you've a talent
You once didn't know that you had?
Have you found something new you can do?
It could be a gift from our Father above
A way that He wants to use you.

Tell someone - a friend - all about it
It helps if together you pray.
If you're not able to use it at once
Keep it fast in your mind don't ignore it
If you do it might go away.

And if it's from God
It's a million to one
He'll want you to use it some day.

Peggy C

Laughter

I could have cried
When I saw them
I could have wept
But I didn't
I laughed instead
And they laughed with me
I looked into their faces
And there were no more tears
There were no tears left
Only joy . . . .

On meting a group of young people with special needs, confined to
wheelchairs, who were brought from their residential home for a short
holiday in our village recently.

Heather Bruyère Watt

God's Gifts

Rose scented gardens and flowering cherries,
Bright Christmas holly smothered with berries,
Heather covered pathways midst craggy Devon tors,
Grazing beasts at roadsides upon the rambling moors,
The sound of birdsong in the dawn,
And distant fields of ripening corn,
Winter, Summer, Autumn, Spring,
The changing seasons His wonders do bring,
The glorious sunsets, star spangled skies,
Aspects of nature, a delight for the eyes,
The tiny babe, a wonder to behold,
'Hush precious one, welcome to the fold',
God granted gifts to man,
To heal, to sing, to plan,
The air we breathe, the land we roam, the sparkling blue sea,
His gifts to us are manifold, forever praised be He.

Ann Madge

This Secluded Place

Flowers in a garden,
A warm Summer's Day,
The golden sun,
The buzzing of the bees,
There are midges in the air,
This feeling of peace and tranquillity,
Beautiful flowers are in abundant availability,
I gather these scented blooms within my arms
And I surrender to this garden's exotic charms,
Then as I slowly wander along its perfumed paths
Where the birds no longer fear my approach,
So tame that I could almost touch them,
This feeling of security and peace
Means so much!
I find a shaded secluded place
To rest a while, and so to vent my feelings,
Could this be Eden, that gently holds me
Within its welcoming warm embrace?

Bah Kaffir

Winter Chill

The perfection of a spider's
Intricate lace-work
Glistens with drops of morning dew
On the hedgerow.
The elms cry in the shadows
Of a fallen landscape
And the world is eerily quiet
In the cold morning sun.
The fog is thick, enveloping
The tired aching earth.
Sorrowful somehow
As though the world was doomed,
And yet painfully beautiful
As a nymph who steals your soul
And crushes it like ice
Black, frosted ice
A reflection of your fear,
Lonely, desolate.
Piercing and biting
As the harsh wind
Tears at a shaky refuge
Merciless, unyielding.
And in the stark
Crystallised environment,
The lone inhabitant
Scuttles free,
Homeless, isolated
In quiet desperation.
In the hollow splintered land
The dying is slow, deliberate,
A spell cast of evil

A helpless cry, brutally ignored
Until finally, with the agony past
The end is over
The chill recedes
And the world is beginning again.

Clare King

Elevation Of The Host

Now blaze, O secret fire in sacred things!
Behold the solemn passion of our sun.
The Saviour treads his way and gilds our wings
As we unite to praise the Holy One.

Since Adam's fall gives life the common leaven,
Dark night and judgement come before the day.
The body which Our Saviour brought from heaven
Will feed and strengthen us upon our way.

Archangels raise the pillar, cloud and flame;
The desert calls and then the promised land.
Afresh we strike the rock of Jesus' name;
The waters part before our pilgrim band.

Sing glory! God now wakes us from our sleep.
His throne is of this world, a royal seat.
His breath and word are hovering o'er the deep.
Praise Father, Son and Holy Paraclete.

David Bowers

Do Appreciate God's Gifts

Good health; good friends; good sight;
Not only to see the mundane, but all the
                world's beauties bright.
The many coloured flowers, and the blossoms
                      on the trees,
And the various shades of the waving leaves.
The beautiful blues of the sea and the sky
And the pure, white clouds gliding by.
The wonderful sunset after a warm bright day
Or the multi-coloured rainbow, after showers
                      came your way.

Some have a better education some a
                brighter brain,
But be glad of what you *have* got, and don't complain!
Everyone with sight sees the colours mentioned
                    above,
And most folk have good families with caring
                  and love.
For those more unfortunate, you should be kind
                    friends and true,
For they need good friends even more than you do!

Marjorie Cowan

Creation

On the first day God made Florence and its treasures.

On the second the people who live there
and take it all for granted.

On Tuesday he made the visitors to appreciate it,
each in his own way but mostly in one another's.

On the fourth day he made the towers and hills, sunlight and air,
colours and mist, river and clouds, eyesight and birds - a busy day.

The next was a day of heavy labour,
raising the Piazzale Michelangelo from the sunken hollow of his
mind to a grand prominence above the city, garlanded with a
circular view and a maze of flowers, perspectives, grass and stone.

On the sixth day God made the magical twilight
between day and night, premonition and history, courage and fear,
nightmare and dream, hunger and strength, peace and war.

And on the Sabbath, at seventeen hundred hours on a day in October,
with his own red sun watching his back from the other side of our
world, He sat on the terrace and gloried in it.

Neville Davis

Searching

Our lives are journeys,
Which never really end.
We search for so much,
But dream for much more.
Our minds search for knowledge,
But should look for wisdom.
Our souls search for peace,
In a confused world.
Our hearts search for love,
At the price of pain.
Our eyes search for perfection,
But it lies deeper within.
Our bodies search for tenderness,
Which is locked too far inside.
We search for so much,
But dream for much more.
However, true contentment,
Is at your door.

M B Chissim

Thanksgiving

I thank my God for the love I had
And the love I had was thine.
And the love we had made the child we had -
The child that was thine and mine.
Now the love I had for the child we had
Was sweet as a grape on the vine
But the love you gave us both was more,
A symbol and a sign.

Now the child is grown and you are gone
Beyond where the known stars shine
And the love you gave from greeting to grave
Not easy to define.
Your unselfish love, your courageous love,
Did our small loves outshine,
And I thank my God for that earthly love
Just touched with the divine.

Catherine Gregory

Sunset

A walk along the riverside
The sunsetting through the pines
Fragrants of new mown hay
Creates a kind of shrine
The serenity of the river
Through the avenue of trees
Their leaves all gently swaying
To the rhythm of the breeze
And fairy lights all twinkling
Through the movement of the leaves
The reflection on the river
Of this tranquil sunset scene
Its mirror image quivering
When a fish decides to rise
And then there is another
And their surface rings entwine
A blackbird breaks the silence
With a twilight melody
All nature and the sunset
In perfect harmony.

D R Blackwell

Anna Lee A Gift From God

Just eighteen years then when I sailed across the China Sea, I had
been sent to a land far away to serve *my queen* and *my country*.

Four good meals a day, little pay, a pack, a gun and sometimes I
would moan, I would dream about my Family and England by Home.

Then one day I saw a pretty Chinese girl shyly smile at me, she never
asked but she hoped I would give her a little food for free.

I had a little chocolate I took it from my pack, it was then I noticed
she shared it with a baby on her back.

Now many times I saw her I called her *Anna Lee*, she always had that
shy beautiful smile that she would give to me.

Every time I saw her I would linger for awhile, just to see her share
with the baby on her back, the baby she had taught to smile.

I had to leave one day I was choked, I could not speak, *Anna Lee* still
gave me that smile as a tear ran down her cheek.

I am sixty three now and I can still see *Anna Lee* the baby and that
beautiful enigmatic smile.

I know now what I did not know then, that was a special gift from
God to me, *Anna Lee*, the Baby, her beautiful shy enigmatic smile
that lives deep in my memory.

Ronald R Astbury

A Never Ending Love

On your very first breath I came into your life
and I was there when you had your first sight.

Your very first thought I was there too,
I have always been there watching over you.
And the very first word that entered your head,
I was also there to hear what you said.

And then when into an adult you grew,
I was there to see you through.
I am always there, close by your side.
My love for you is stronger than the tide.

Never ever think that you are alone
because you are never on your own.
I'm nearer to you than you realise,
Although you can't see me with your eyes.

Be still and listen to the small voice in you
and you will meet a friend so true.
Just pray for guidance from above
and I'll be there with all my love.

A love that's deeper than the sea
and that's the way it will always be.
Never ever doubt these words of mine
because I'm with you always 'til the end of time.

Robert Beach

Tears

Tears from inner reservoirs,
Prickling the back of my eyes,
Blurring my vision, wetting my cheeks.
Salty rivulets stream forth.
Of what purpose are these tears of mine?
I often ask the question, as unprovoked they flow.
Tears like this are a gift from God,
In times of great joy, tears pour forth,
As though joy spilled over into a water fall.
Cascading over life's obstacles in abundance
In times of great sorrow, tears pour forth,
Thawing the painful frozen areas of my life,
Which adhere to and mar my being.
In times of affliction tears pour forth,
Bringing with them trust and gentle healing.
Washing away all that which is not of God.
When moved by others grief, tears pour forth,
Helpless to do anything to help constructively,
My heart aches, as I am present to their need.
It is as though in some mysterious way,
Their suffering is shared - my tears are your compassion.
Yet still I question the timing of these tears,
For seldom can I explain their reason, at their point of flow.
I see others looking, some in disbelief, disowning,
Others look with deep concern, caring, what is the trouble?
How do I explain these tears of joy and compassion?
I say I feel happy and yet still my tears flow.
I say please leave me be, just let my tears flow.
For I know that whatever their cause, flooding over,
I feel cleansed, refreshed, enervated.
Yet I feel concerned for those concerned for me!
Do they understand my tears? My gift from God?
Soggy though it be, or do my tears affect them,
In ways I would not wish to incur?

Help my own acceptance of this healing gift,
Enlighten those around me, assuring them that -
When my tears flow, they need only be accepted,
I ask no more than that, let understanding later follow,
Today I ask, just sit a while with me.

Teresa Booth

A Treasured Gift

Strolling hand in hand
eyes drawn skywards
wispy white clouds
dancing by.

Talk turns to
days long ago.
When love was so young
and hope sprung eternal.

Life has been good
we have not parted.
Growing old together
holding hands of leather.

Oh what memories
we have stored.
Giving eternal pleasure
with each measure.

As each dawn breaks
I give thanks to the Lord
for the treasured gift
that is you.

Keith Furner

God's Gifts

Faith - to keep us believing
when doubts come crowding in.
Hope - to keep us going on
when we feel like giving in.
Love - to give us comfort
as we go on our way.
These Gifts of God sustain us
today and every day.

Edna Cosby

Wonder Of Nature

Here and there the birds do sing
Blackbird - Thrush and fair Lapwing.
Constantly their tunes they play
Until the end ing of the day.
But best of all near eventide
It's then they sing out with great pride
Heralding the night's approach
Watching clouds cross sky encroach.
Yet again with morns first light
Renew their song - what sound - what sight.
A God who gave this life to me
Also gave the plant and tree.
Will it be there for evermore?
Just the same as it was of yore?
With constant change before my eye
May it be so until I die.

D Adams

One God

I gave life to all of you
The God of Gentile and of Jew.
On your table I lay a feast
The God of both man and beast.

You must rest of the seventh day
If you commit sin then you will pay.
Never take another man's wife
A gift to you of eternal life.

Take your neighbours by the hand
Share with each this my land.
Put aside all of your wealth
Just be true unto thy self.

The cruel waters I will still
But you must never kill.
With obedience you must come to me
Then in Heaven a home you see.

I am the God of James and John
My Kingdom will just go on.
All the things Moses did do
This day I give them to you.

Colin Allsop

A Little Flower

I am just a little flower
A blossom white as snow,
I am taken for granted
Everywhere I grow.

I am very content
To grow in my little way,
Closing my petals at sunset
Displaying them by day.

I do not have the splendour
Of a rose or daffodil
Nor claim their fragrant beauty
Or majestic apparel.

I may not be chosen
As the flower of the season,
You see, I am so little,
That must be the reason.

At times weeds envelope me
It's hard to stay alive
I may be trodden on
Yet somehow I survive!

Do not be deluded
By my fragile frame,
I am endowed with flower power
- Daisy is my name.

I am just a little flower
Created by divine love,
My greatness lies in my littleness,
A gift from God above.

Monica Docherty

Resurrection

Sometimes in an
early morning in May,
one can glimpse the restorative
powers of heaven
and cast off the decaying body
in the shimmering azure
of a peaceful bluebell wood.
The intoxicating perfume
fills the senses,
the quietness
renews the spirit.
A tranquillised hour.
Lost, all alone, enraptured,
no other sound,
no other soul
no other consciousness
an incense bowl,
encapsulated in love
made possible by the renewal
of the dead bulb
into full scented flower.

Elizabeth Peirce

Jealous

Hey seagull - show off
At your best today
In squally rain and tumbling wind flying
Stunts crazy
You're not so daring in freefall
I've trusted jets to rush me
Lower than your pretty dipping wavespray games

Yes I tried high to race the wind
And feel God's blue drive me free
Grounded now I watch your fun
Blasted wind - Tearing rain
Burst my lungs with piercing gravity
I'd join you honest but you should see
My cold feet soaked in logic

Eileen Fawcett

The Gift Of Love

What a wonderful gift is love
To receive it and to give,
It must be sent from God above
To help the way we live.

To show people that we care
And lend a helping hand,
Warm feelings we can share
And kind words to tell them we
Understand.

J Bell

Daughter of Abraham

(Luke 13 v 10-17)
(Dedicated to Marianne and friends at
Upper Tooting Methodist Prayer Fellowship)

I went to the synagogue
On the Sabbath day.
With my stick, and all bent over
I went along to pray.

I was so crouched over
I couldn't see the sky,
Or the look on people's faces
As they passed by.

I had a problem walking
The pain was so great,
In my back and shoulders
I couldn't stand up straight.

I was healed by Jesus
On the Sabbath day.
But the ruler of the synagogue
Had to have his say.

'The Sabbath is for resting
Work should not be done.
Healing is for other days
Not 'till Sabbath's gone.'

The Lord of the Sabbath
Spoke to his surprise.
'You would release your ox today
Let this lady rise.'

The crowd were so happy
A miracle they've seen.
My bent back is now as straight
As it's ever been.

A daughter of Abraham
I shall always be.
Thank you Lord Jesus
You set your people free.

Christine Webster

Gifts From God

God gave me gifts of children three
I took his gifts unquestioning
'til like all Gods he jealously
removed one precious gift from me.

It seemed He never could forgive
my arrogant pride in their pure grace,
The price I'd not yet fully paid
was called upon me to embrace.

Our fragile lives his to command
He sought to take my other child
but paused, relented what he'd planned,
reversed and stayed his hand a while.

He let me keep my second child
tho' proved at closing of the day,
that what the Lord gives as a gift
He surely can snatch away.

Barbara Davies

A Time For Everything

A time of gladness
Fills one's heart full of joy
No matter what befalls during the day
Gladness will prevail

A time of sadness
Will enter one's life
With an echo that clings
But sadness can be quickly removed

A time of faithfulness
Is a gift that one must harbour
Because it is a good feeling
And faithfulness is a great healer

A time of great alarm
Can be blotted out at once
By tethering one's mind to true reality
Alerted alarm can be averted

A time of brightness
Will put sunshine into one's heart
Build a temple of love around yourself
Brightness will enhance your sight

A time of sincerity
Will enter one's life
For eternity if one will let it
Sincerity is wonderful

A time of everlasting love
Will enter into one's soul
A glittering light so very bright
Everlasting love brings for ever happiness.

Alma Montgomery Frank

A Friend-In-Need

When you're feeling lonely
And the days seem long
And nobody comes to see you
And everything's gone wrong,
I'll be there for you to turn to
As I always said I would.

When you're feeling ill
And life seems hard to bear
And you're full of aches and pains
And nobody seems to care,
I'll be there for you to turn to
As I always said I would.

When you're feeling hopeless
And tempted to despair,
And there's nobody to talk to
Because there's no-one there,
I'll be there for you to turn to
As I always said I would.

Beryl Johnson

Millennium

And will He come, as promised long ago,
Our risen Lord, in glory and in might,
Yet still the gracious Friend His friends would know?

So hard it is for us, whose faith is slow,
And still must ask, as learning dazzles sight,
'And will He come, as promised long ago?'

Our simple forbears simpler trust would show;
Just overhead they pictured heaven's gate,
Whence came the gracious Friend His friends would know.

As this millennium comes, will wisdom grow?
May we indeed receive Him, though so late?
And will He come, as promised long ago?

Our risen Lord, from whom all truth shall flow,
Two thousand years have passed! Do we still wait,
Or will He come, as promised long ago
And still the gracious Friend His friends would know?

Kathleen M Hatton

The Millennium

'A thousand ages in the sight
Are like an evening gone' (Hymn)

Two evenings since you, Lord, were born
and died and rose, so then
another evening turns the date -
short term since earth began -
and shorter still the annals are
since first lived on by man.
What will the future minutes bring
to all the human race?
And will your teaching claim the earth
to bring your father's grace?
Ancient of days, O Lord of all
grant this dark night be done;
short as the watch that ends the night,
then grant a rising sun.

Owen Edwards

A Dream

Last night I dreamed I walked in Heaven
but how it was I did not see.
There may have been the gates of pearl
and walls of solid gold.
I did not raise my eyes to look
for at my side you also walked
and your strong hand was warm in mine.

Sweetly we communed and talked
untroubled by constraints of time.
What we said was nothing new
to be remembered afterward.
How you looked I did not see
nor where we went give heed.

But weightless was our walk,
sweet harmony our talk,
and firm and warm your hand.

Jennifer Hashmi

Is Sunday For Sale

Sitting her in the queue
has the time come for the Sunday pew
It's now a Sunday ritual but there is no God about
one thing's for sure the Sunday punters about.

The gates open the crowds rush in,
are we committing the almighty sin.
The Bible is nowhere to be seen
As the bargain hunters begin to pray
the bargain, is their salvation for the day.

The bargain basket gets passed about
is this really helping God out.
Is this the modern way.
We should spend our Sunday
I think God is the best bargain of the day

It's free

J Gallagher

The Millennium

The Millennium would be soon here?
A lot are looking forward to have good cheer
Some would be Eating, Drinking and having fun
But we all must think, we cannot Run

That is not what it is all about?
From the past, and present, we on our way out
All the Years we see, things are getting worst to me?
The Wars, Disaster, Hate, and Pain,
Looking back what really we gain?

We far advance in our living?
Seen things we never Dream of having,
And yet we are Living in Fear?
Wonder every minute who would be there
No safe place here on Earth
At times some wonder is this a Mystery, or Myth

But think what we can achieve,
If we cultivate Love for others, and their need?
We all are one no matter Colour, or Race
It is here on Earth, we all should have space.

Nothing is wrong with the Earth, we have all we need
It is those that comes along and spoil it with Greed?
Bring back Hanging, some would like this
All those that committed Murder, should be Hang, and never Miss.

As the Millennium approaches, we should think of Unity, and peace
It can only come if we increase -
Do to others, as we would like others to do to you?
If we all try, this is not very hard to do.

No one knows, what the Future holds
But one thing, we all have our Doors
As we open it let us not forget
To do anything, that we will regret.

F Yankee

Christ's Millennium: Earth, God's Footstool

By sun and moon and starshine
And ever angels' glow,
The dearest light of Christendom
Comes from the Heart we know
That beat in Man two thousand years
Before this helpless time,
And all the lights it made since then
Join at Millennium's chime.

Push back the dark. Come mighty dawn,
Illumination's birth.
Let mercy, justice, peace and love
Invest a shining Earth.
He who leads us through to God
Will take each grubbing hand,
Steadying still our shaking steps
When on the brink we stand
Of Millennium's golden nexus,
Where time and faith unite
And once more wait in radiant hope
For Man to set aright
the agonised thought of ages,
Mistakes of minds unlit.
Then shall the Earth return through Christ,
God's Footstool, clean and fit.

I H Pyves

Christian Thoughts On The Millennium

Two thousand years have passed since the miracle birth
Of the baby Jesus, God's gift to folk on earth,
No room in the inn, so born in a stable stall,
From early life, he realised that Love surpasses all.

The Immaculate Conception must surely be
The most amazing miraculous mystery,
Born of Virgin Mary, He was her earthly son,
The wonder of it all, He was God's chosen One.

He practised what He preached, a lifetime doing good,
His message bright and clear, that people understood,
It has been claimed that in all of history's span,
The world was changed forever by this one man.

He said, 'Other sheep I have which are not of this fold.'
We should remember now our Lord's wisdom of old,
No time like the present to make some amends
And greet other faiths as our millennium friends.

He suffered death upon the Cross, a cross of shame,
In agony, He called for help, but no help came.
On Easter day, He rose from death, freed from His grave,
By miracle His Father moved, His holy Son to save.

Christians awake, declare your faith and celebrate,
On this most welcome and long awaited date,
With greetings, prayers with praise, and most joyful singing,
Bands will be playing and church bells will be ringing.

Christ in God's realm now reigns, forever glorious,
Triumphant over sin and death, ever victorious,
God's kingdom will endure, He has the Masterplan,
His Universe of wonder, beyond the world of man.

George V Goodchild

Just Be
(A psalm for the Millennium)

All we ever have is past.
We might not be in future;
And the present does not last.

Indeed, there is no present.
No sooner is the future,
Than it promptly was the past.

So, think not of tomorrow.
Nor bother about today.
Just be grateful for the past.

Be not concerned with questions -
The Who's the How's or the Why's?
All are guesses, whims or lies.

Just be grateful for the past.
Take it as a simple fact -
We have been and so we are.

If you wonder where you are,
Since there is no place to be.
Wonder. In eternity.

Be thankful.
Praise the Lord.
And just be.

Bob Davies

What Is Ahead

As we approach the new millennium
Do you wonder what is ahead
Will we face a new future
Or had we just as well be dead

Will we all stop fighting
Will we care for fellow man
Will we care for planet earth
And show love the best we can

Is peace going to be real
Can we feel secure
Can we go out at night
And no more lock the door.

Can we move around freely
And children play in the street
Can they talk to everyone
Including the stranger that they meet

The time ahead is to be just so
We pray for it to come true
We ask God's will on earth as in heaven
And he has promised to make all new

He will bring peace to earth
No man can bring this about
Only God's kingdom can do that
When he sorts all things out

Gone will be crime fear and war
Gone the gloom of what is ahead
Every day will be good to be alive
And to thank Jehovah God that you're not dead

Mark Llewellyn

Millennium Hymn

Lord of Heaven, Lord of earth,
'Shrined in Glory and in Love
You sent Your Son - our Saviour's birth
Angels singing up above.
Now we praise You, bless You, thank You,
Bow before You and embrace
All the blessings You have given us
In Your boundless, wondrous Grace.

Your Honour, Wisdom, Power, Glory,
Thro' the generations gone
Echo in our hearts for ever,
Linger through the days to come.
For we need Your Love and Guidance
As we face the future years
Show us all Your breathless beauty
To dispel our fears and tears.

As the Century passes over
And the shadows fall away
Help us so to trust for ever
And to love You day by day.
We have Peace and Consolation
And Your Guiding Hand proclaim
As we face our expectations
We will glorify Your Name.

Sanctify our best endeavours
As we move from age to age
Our promises ensure that never
Shall we spoil the brand new page
For the finger writing on it
Will be circled by Your Love
In the path of Peace we follow
And the blessings of the Dove.

Hallelujah to our Father
Hallelujah to our King
Praises rise to God in Glory
As with all one voice we sing.
Though we walk in trepidation
We will follow Your dear Son
We have hope and blest assurance
Through the new Millennium!

Mollie D Earl

A New Millennium

The year of 1999 is nearing the end,
looking back it has not been too bad.
It will be like losing a very dear old friend,
there have been happy moments and some sad.

The new Millennium will also soon begin,
will we grow richer or maybe poor.
We cannot guess what it will be,
we will be a year older that's for sure!

It is the final year of a dying century,
a century of great events and drastic changes.
Two great wars, death and injury,
exploration of deserts and mountain ranges.

This is also the year of a dying millennium.
How much have we changed in a 1000 years?
War after war, and so on ad infinitum.
Plead for them to stop, but who hears

We look forward with hope to the new year,
in the hope that once more we find love,
love of life, of God, and with minds clear,
and that black and white live hand in glove.

Joyce G Shinn

Monument

Two thousand years have passed since Hope was born
But what has mankind in all it's wisdom done?
Not Peace and Plenty shared throughout the globe
(The wish of One who died in homespun robe)
But War and Famine half the world have filled,
when children and young girls are raped and killed
by those whose evil minds are filled with hate and lust
who, when they go, leave burning homes and corpses in the dust

To celebrate the last two thousand years of raised intelligence
our politicians, in their great wisdom,
devised a wondrous plan and sparing no expense
decided that a monument be built to man
and all his marvellous achievements.
Not plans to stop all strife, for that made *too* much sense,
but a large edifice that, within a few short years,
would rust, decay and sink into the ground,
a ground made soft with our frustrated tears.

No Crystal Palace this, but a large round plastic dome
a huge, curved, empty and quite ugly thing
filled with hot air, a spiked inverted cup
(much like the heads of those who thought the concept up.)
And surely nothing about which to shout,
which cost more money than we care to think about.

While millions of pot bellied babes sit quiet and stare,
with huge, pathetic eyes, filled with despair,
at nothing, as they die of thirst, for there is naught to drink.
Because what could be spent to sink, not just a single well
but thousands more, to bring relief from grief,
has all be wasted, profligately thrown away beyond belief
and sunk into a hollow and quite useless shell.

David G W Garde

A Millennium Prayer

Strutting and fretting at the Gateway of 'Millennium Three',
The countdown from the primary one - 'The birth of Christianity',
In quest of a light to walk safely into the unknown,
I wafted silent prayers Heavenwards to make my fears known
To *Him*, Alpha and Omega, Repository of our Trust, -
Though diverse in nomenclature in every ethnic cult,
Thou doth connote singularity, - not plurality,
And in our human reckoning, as one single Deity,
In this symbolic moment in time, we who live in time,
Are privileged to converge on *Thee*, who art outside Time -
Our only link between the Past, Present, and the Future -
With someone or something beyond the 'Here and Now' cloister!
So, for emancipation in the next Millennium, Let's *Pray*:-
That we be good stewards, keeping the *Earth* in pristine array:
That there be *Peace* on *Earth*, and Goodwill towards men and
                                                        Nations:
That we display surfeit of *Love* and exercise Patience:
That the Lord's Goodness and Mercy follow us throughout Life:
That our sins be forgiven, when others to pardon, we strive:
That we witness the emergence of a New Heaven on Earth:
Where *Satan* is bound for a thousand years, to mankind's mirth!
                                        - *Amen* -

Welch Jeyaraj Balasingam

172

Changes Needed

I would like to see in the Millennium
some worthwhile alterations
Where homeless are given a place to live
to end their sad frustration

I pray this drug addiction
at last begins to wane
Where the young all start to realise
this life means only pain.

I hope that all the unemployed
find jobs to suit their station
As life can be an empty shell
in a jobless situation.

Society can only but be good
in healthy circumstances
This is what life is all about
us giving youth their chances

Lachlan Taylor

I Wonder

I wonder what Mary thought when the Holy Ghost paid her a visit.
I wonder if she thought 'How am I to tell Joseph and is it
true? Why me? I shall have to wait and see
and trust in the Lord if it is to be.'

I wonder what Joseph thought when he came in from work
and Mary said 'Joseph. I have to talk
to you and tell you about today.
I have been chosen in a very strange way.
The Lord spoke to me and the Holy Ghost
has visited me and it is most
extraordinary what has been done
for God has chosen me to bear his son.'

I wonder if Joseph thought 'Why not me
to be given the seed for me to be
the father so the child would also be mine,
a true and direct descendant of David's line?'

I wonder why so many women were destined to mourn
for their sons who had been born
at the same time as Jesus and all were slaughtered
by Herod's men as he had ordered.
How dreadful that all those children were slain.
Imagine the mothers' suffering and pain.

I wonder what happened to Joseph and why
he wasn't there when Jesus was going to die.
He should have been there to comfort his wife
when she knew that her son would lose his life.

I wonder what Mary would have thought had she known
that from early Christendom she'd have renown;
be accepted by the converted and take the place
of the goddess of Nature, the pagan race
had worshipped throughout all their time on earth,
knowing nothing of God and a Saviour's birth,
belief in Christ and a certainty
that people would live for eternity
after they died, as it seems proved
to those who followed him whom he loved.

About all these things I wonder
and over them all I ponder.

Muriel Woolven

Man And Earth Redeemed

Cursed Man

In city theatres ticket-holders thrash
Through black hose web tunnel,
Serpent river lobby,
Through darkness
Descending to an
Underground snakepit gallery.
Handed white neon crepe
Head embalming wrap.
In the theatre-canyon of human glow-worms --
Demonic actors delight.

The play and players, Blue Man Group,
A roving villainous band of
Death peddlers.
Garbage sucking vacuums.
Human sewer geysers spewing vomit art.
White eyes stare from blue frozen faces.
Cold moons in black winter skies.

Miles of luminous toilet streamers
Dragged 'cross, rolling over, encoiling
Heads and shoulders.
Strangle and stifle the unsuspecting --
The mindless, laughing, living dead,
The seeing blind, themselves the play.

Stage emperor actors scoff.
Their hollow laugh unheard by human ears.
The just One will silence them a million years.

One child sees the evil intent.
Feels the terror,
Flees the doom.
Crawling under
Rolling waves
Of mummy wrap
She escapes.

Cursed Earth

Slithering, pulsing Kudzu vines,
Black-green endless Ilydra snakes
Smother Kentucky Bluegrass, Indian Paintbrush, daisy.
Towering oak and maple canopies, that
Once shaded summer lambs and calves,
Now Kudzu claws grasp
And pull down low.
Limbs wrapped with billowy bat wings,
Kudzu leaves coffin tree and earth,
Silencing, forever, bubbling brooks.

Wild, sweet, pink river valley roses,
Once, deer nibbled.
Now smouldering decay --
Incense to some demented demon.
There is a better way.

On country roads,
Where children skipped, school bags swinging,
Between verdant pastures
An army of ravenous vipers advance.
Subterranean tentacles weave
A black web 'neath abandoned farmlands wide.

Up orchard hillsides, down rambling riverbanks
Cows grazed and mooed, and goats gambolled --
Now snakepit silence shrouds.

Vines encoil deserted farmhouse porches,
Turn wicker rockers into motionless spectres.
Tall windows, where lace curtains
By gentle breezes blew'
Now black tendrils clog,
Walling out light and warmth.
Inky, eeries stillness now here
Lazy dog days buzzed, hummed and croaked.
Peepers crushed, ground choir hushed
Forever.

Blessed Vine Of Life

His earth crown, a thorny vine.
His brow blood trickling o'er lips forgiing.
All vines His death transforms.
Our cleansing, a healing joy and peace becomes.

Cursed earth, cursed man.
Apart from Him death fills the land.
And our souls, and our souls.

But out of our darkness, into His light.
One of our smotheirng, smouldering shadowy caves,
Into His redeeming shining streams.
From Him eternal life, love, joy and truth cascade.
Valley Lily, Sharon Rose,
Dew mists from His dawning

He is the vine.
He is the life.
Apart from Him, deceived, we perish.
In Him, gloriously we live.
And behold both man and earth redeemed.

Nina Helene